BONES HOOKS

BONES
Pioneer Negro Cowboy
HOOKS

By Bruce G. Todd

PELICAN PUBLISHING COMPANY
GRETNA 2005

The word "Pelican" and the depiction of a pelican are trademarks
of Pelican Publishing Company, Inc., and are registered in the
U.S. Patent and Trademark Office.

Library of Congress Cataloging-in-Publication Data

Todd, Bruce G.
   Bones Hooks : pioneer Negro cowboy / by Bruce G. Todd.
      p. cm.
   Includes bibliographical references (p.   ) and index.
   ISBN-13: 978-1-58980-294-0 (pbk. : alk. paper)
   1. Hooks, Bones, 1867-1951. 2. African American cowboys—Pecos
River Valley (N.M. and Tex.)—Biography. 3. Cowboys—Pecos River
Valley (N.M. and Tex.)—Biography. 4. African American pioneers—
Pecos River Valley (N.M. and Tex.)—Biography. 5. Frontier and pio-
neer life—Pecos River Valley (N.M. and Tex.) 6. Ranch life—Pecos
River Valley (N.M. and Tex.) 7. Pecos River Valley (N.M. and Tex.)—
Biography. 8. African Americans—Texas, West—Biography. I. Title.

   F392.P3T63 2005
   976.4'06'092—dc22

                                                              2004027736

Printed in the United States of America

Published by Pelican Publishing Company, Inc.
1000 Burmaster Street, Gretna, Louisiana 70053

To Mathew ("Bones") Hooks, for the honor for which he stood despite the hatred in such uncompromising times

And for two friends whose names cannot be mentioned. M. H. encouraged me from the outset to succeed with the book, and G. J. M. D. stood with me in my personal hard times. I am greatly indebted to both of them.

Contents

Preface

This book began out of the African-American Oral History Project of Potter County in the Texas Panhandle in an effort to document black pioneer history. As the wealth of information was collected it became increasingly obvious that much of this information should be published. One story that came from this project was that of a black cowboy and pioneer, Mathew ("Bones") Hooks. Although Bones Hooks was widely recognized not only in the Texas Panhandle but in West Texas, Colorado, and Oklahoma too, and had been the subject of numerous interviews, a book-length biography of this astonishing man was never written until now.

Monica Hilling, a former professor of English and French at West Texas A&M, was the first to encourage writing such a book. The next was Rev. Jess Cortez, of black and Hispanic heritage, who supported the project from the outset and was as forthright and open as anyone I interviewed. Another person to impress upon me that my research in regional black history should be published was Dr. Charles Townsend, the author of Bob Wills' life story, *San Antonio Rose,* and formerly a professor of history at West Texas A&M. Further support came from Walt Davis, president of the Panhandle-Plains Historical Museum, and Lisa Lambert and Betty Bustos of the Archives department. Betty Bustos was always willing and able to help out on this project. A special thanks goes to the Amarillo Public Library System, which furnished photos, newspaper articles, and advice. The entire staff was helpful, but particularly Art Bort, John Birchfield, Kay Johnson, Katie Anthony, Rob Groman, Greg Thomas, Sara Clark, Lana Hughes, Kevin Hill, Judith Sample, and Gayle Brown, who was responsible for indexing many years of the Amarillo newspapers.

However, the most important and pivotal assistance came from the black community and specifically Charles Kemp, the former president of the Black Cultural Center of Amarillo. He put me in contact with those whose parents and grandparents were some of the first blacks not only in Amarillo but the Texas Panhandle. Equally important were Juell Shorten Nutter and Charles Warford. Juell Nutter, whose parents were pioneer and community leaders, has long been considered the historian of her people in Amarillo and her research was invaluable to this book. Charles Warford came to Amarillo as a child in the mid 1930s and, like Charles Kemp, knew Bones Hooks as a boy. Charles Warford is a walking history book and recalled people and events with great clarity. I am grateful, as I relied heavily on his guidance in understanding Bones Hooks. I owe a great deal of thanks to these individuals, as well as those too numerous to name, including the dozens of men and women interviewed in the African-American Oral History Project. Without them, the story of Mathew ("Bones") Hooks could not have been written.

Introduction

Bill Pickett, the famous black cowboy otherwise known as the "Dusky Demon," was elected to the Cowboy Hall of Fame in 1971, and he was more than deserving, as many black cowboys still are. Yet there is one black cowboy whose career surpasses that of most, regardless of color, and who ought to be in the Great Westerners Hall of Fame but is not. His name is Mathew ("Bones") Hooks.

Bones, as he was simply known all over West Texas, the Panhandle, and the Plains, was destined to be a cowboy—and not just a cowboy but a bronc buster with no equal. He left home at the age of nine to pursue that dream, and he rode his first wild horse in North Texas when he was twelve. By the time he was a scrawny fifteen-year-old, he had traveled to the rugged Pecos country of West Texas, where he made a name far and wide as a great bronc rider. He soon went into partnership with a white friend, Tommy Clayton, and had his own brand, *B,* presumably standing for Bones. He worked most of the ranches of that region. By his own admission, he was never an all-around cowhand, such as the great Jim Perry of the XIT Ranch, but a specialist. He went wherever his bronc-riding services led him.

In 1886 he arrived in Clarendon and was in the

Panhandle during the terrible blizzards of the 1886-87 winter. He worked as wrangler and bronc buster for the formidable pioneer and trailblazer Col. Charles Goodnight on more than one occasion. Goodnight never told Bones how much he appreciated his skills, but he spread the news all over the Panhandle to his rancher friends, building him an even stronger reputation. Bones went back and forth from the Panhandle to the Pecos for a number of years until 1896, when he settled in the Panhandle. After marrying in 1900, he retired from bronc busting. That same year he traveled to Denver to the world rodeo that was already established as a great Western event, but he was denied participation because of his color. This was the first time that blacks were kept out of the sport since it had become popular in the early 1880s. He returned to the Panhandle and tried ranching in New Mexico for a few years. By 1909 he had taken a job on the Santa Fe Railroad as a Pullman porter. A year later, he was coaxed out of retirement to ride an outlaw horse that no one else could. A friend and pioneer rancher thought Bones ought to try. The event happened in the Panhandle in Pampa, Texas, with a number of witnesses on hand. At the age of forty-two Bones pulled off this amazing feat. Drawings and poems were created in his honor, and his name spread as far away as New York The great bronc rider who had not been allowed to participate in the Denver rodeo was praised by the world bronco champion, "Booger Red" (Samuel Thomas Privett), who told the world that whatever he could ride in a saddle, Bones could ride bareback.

In the years that followed, Bones' great prowess on a horse was memorialized through more poems, songs, and, of course, stories around campfires. In 1926, just before one of the cowboy reunions in Amarillo, four old cowmen were discussing who was the greatest bronc rider of all time. Several names were mentioned, including Chuck Yarborough, who reportedly won a $250 bet with Buffalo Bill. The *Amarillo Daily News* ran an article based on the cowmen's conversation titled, "Old Bones, a Pioneer Negro Porter on Santa Fe Called Best Bronc Rider on the Plains." In the article, one of the old cowmen spoke up after hearing all of the other arguments. He said, "I reckon Old Bones is the best rider ever to straddle a horse on the Plains. . . . Yes, Bones is a Negro, but those who know him say he is undoubtedly one of the best riders the United States has ever known. . . . I guess Old Bones is the best bronc buster the Panhandle has ever known."

If Bones' story ended with his cowboy achievements, it would have been a great story, but Bones was much more than an old cowboy. He became a leader of his people, a civic and social worker, a Western-style philosopher, and a builder of character and self-esteem. He helped organize the first black church in the Panhandle while he was still breaking wild horses near Clarendon, and after he moved to Amarillo he quickly established himself as a leader there. He was on hand when the Mt. Zion Missionary Baptist Church was organized and may have helped establish the Fred Douglass Elementary School. He built a Negro town just outside of Amarillo's city limits that was annexed by the city, he erected a community center named Pioneer Hall, and he was prominent in establishing the area's first black high school. He founded the Colored Panhandle Pioneer Club, was one of the original members of the Negro Chamber of Commerce, and founded the Dogie Club, an organization for young boys that gained widespread recognition and praise.

As impressive as this list of accomplishments is, Bones' achievements did not end here. He used his name to raise money for various black causes and traveled all over the country on a Santa Fe Railroad pass representing his race in Panhandle history and other black accomplishments. In addition, he proudly carried on the old cowboy tradition of giving honor to whom honor was due by presenting a lone white flower to individuals or a bouquet of flowers to families and groups, first to pioneers and later to those who contributed to a better society. The first honored were West Texas and Panhandle pioneers; later he extended the tradition to dignitaries around the world, including Franklin Roosevelt and Winston Churchill. Bones did everything he could to make things better for his race and was often called a "peacemaker" in that he tried to close the gap between the races. He personally was not subjected to much prejudice and crossed the race barrier with ease. He lived a lot in the white world but not for personal gain. He used all of his influence for his people, but sometimes his ways were not understood. He belonged to several white organizations such as the Western Cowpunchers Association, the Old Settlers Reunion, and the XIT Association. He was the first and, at the time, only black member of the Panhandle-Plains Historical Society and was often interviewed for a column in the Amarillo newspaper called "Bones Bits," recollecting the pioneer days.

No, Bones' story does not read like that of other black cowboys. His story is unique, indeed. The life he led and the things he accomplished were nothing less than amazing when one considers the era in which he lived and the attitude toward blacks in general. Perhaps that is why his name lives on even to this day in the Texas Panhandle.

BONES HOOKS

PART I

CHAPTER 1

The Early Years

Mr. Donald drove some cattle to Henrietta and left me there with them. I stayed and called Henrietta home. Well, it was just before this that I got the nickname "Bones." . . . I ain't never been able to get rid of that name yet and I'm seventy years old.

—Bones Hooks

On an early March day in 1910, a slender black man, approximately five feet and seven inches tall, who was one of the legendary cowboys on the High Plains, made a truly historic ride on an outlaw horse. This particular black cowboy was not as obscure as many black cowboys had become due to being written out of history by white writers aimed at white readers, and he continued to be an integral part of the real West. His name was Mathew ("Bones") Hooks, and this was his final great ride on a worthy wild horse, a horse that was as much an expression of the Old West as was the bronc rider himself. This ride was going to be documented and go down in history, but more importantly, it was going to cement the bronc rider's reputation for all time.

"The Ride," as it was simply known, occurred when Bones was past the prime of a bronc buster, at the age of forty-two.

He had been retired since 1900. "The Ride" was not planned as a publicity stunt such as Buffalo Bill's Wild West Show might have planned. Actually, it was put in motion a couple of days earlier on a Santa Fe passenger train between Amarillo and Pampa, Texas. Bones was employed as a Pullman porter, a position he had taken the previous year. One day as he was working this train, some old cattlemen were aboard whom Bones knew, one of them quite well. They were discussing an outlaw horse that nobody could ride. Bones lingered nearby, dusting the seats so he could listen to the conversation. As he later recalled, "I hate to miss any horse talk."[1]

One of the men was J. D. Jefferies of Clarendon, a pioneer rancher and civic leader for whom Bones had worked as a wrangler. Naturally, Bones couldn't resist breaking into their conversation. The cattlemen, except for Jefferies, were certain that no one could ride the outlaw horse. Jefferies suggested to Bones that he ride it. Bones discussed it with the cattlemen, and a purse of twenty-five dollars was put up if he could ride the outlaw. Bones agreed, but more for the challenge than the money. He said, "Well, you tell him [the owner, Mart Davidson] to have his horse at the depot in Pampa the day after tomorrow and I'll ride him."[2]

Jefferies soon disembarked, but two days later, on March 12, the train that Bones was working rolled into the depot at Pampa, about sixty miles northeast of Amarillo, and the outlaw horse and its owner were waiting for him. A number of others were on hand, too. They had heard that the great Bones Hooks was going to ride the meanest of all horses. News also spread throughout the train as to what was about to take place. The passengers were filled with excitement as Bones took off his square porter's hat and white jacket. He was already wearing his boots and spurs and looked forward to this thrill and challenge. The passengers hung out the windows to see a real live bronc buster in action. For some it was a first-time experience and one they were not likely to forget.

Bones quickly appraised the animal. In his youth, how many times had he rode an outlaw horse that they said no one could ride? It was too many to count. Was he now too old? He would soon know. Bowlegged from many years of straddling a horse, he put a foot in the stirrup, gripped the reins, climbed on top, and the wild ride began. The horse flailed and bucked, twisted and turned, but he stayed in the saddle, reminiscent of his former days of greatness, until he rode that wild horse to a standstill. Applause and congratulations poured forth, and he was as gracious as always. He collected the purse and immediately sent a wire to his friend, Jefferies: *Outlaw rode. Collected money. Gone east.* As he returned to his position on the train and put on his hat and jacket, the passengers looked at the Negro porter in a different way. They patted him on the back and offered him the respect that he had known before the turn of the century, when he was one of the most admired bronc riders on the High Plains. But nothing else had changed.[3]

Many times prior to "The Ride," Bones had been the topic of conversation among old cowhands and "The Ride" just fueled that talk even more, especially at the cowboy and pioneer reunions in the Panhandle. "The Ride" was the talk around campfires and just about anywhere old cowhands got together. It spotlighted a dying way of life. Talk of "The Ride" reached as far away as Chicago and New York, and later Paul Laune, a New York artist but a Texan by birth, immortalized Bones through vivid sketches of the event. After the famous ride, he wasn't criticized anymore but was given due respect as one of the greatest bronc riders of all time in an area dominated by whites. But perhaps most importantly, "The Ride" opened doors for Bones that were not open to any other black person in the West and probably the entire country. "The Ride" was one of the things that elevated Bones' status to near that of whites in the region and it formed the base from which he would become a civic and social leader of his race.

His story, however, does not begin in Amarillo, nor even the Texas Panhandle. It begins in Robertson County, in East Texas, where he was born on November 3, 1867. He said that he was born in old Orangeville, but records indicate that an Orangeville never existed in Robertson County, although an Owensville did from 1859 to 1870. Owensville was the county seat for awhile, but when the H. & T. C. Railway extended to Calvert and did not come to Owensville, the old county seat became isolated and Calvert eventually became the county seat. Owensville finally turned into pasture and farmlands, until there was little evidence that it ever existed.[4]

Bones was born to Alex and Annie Hooks, who were believed to have been slaves of Cullin (Carlin) Hooks of Bowie County in Northeast Texas, about twenty-five miles west of Texarkana. This is where the town of Hooks, Texas, later grew up. Emancipation came to black Texans more than two years after Pres. Abraham Lincoln's proclamation on January 1, 1863. The news was slow in coming to Texas slaves and when it did arrive, the war was already over. Their news of freedom arrived on June 19, 1865, a date that is unique in Texas history but that is now celebrated annually far and wide, known as Juneteenth. Like many ex-slaves, Alex took his former slaveholder's last name.

However, as a slave under the Hooks family, Alex quickly proved his intelligence and was segregated from the field hands. He became an "errand and library boy" and was taught to read and write so that he was able to carry out his responsibilities more than adequately. The education that Alex acquired was going to play an important role not only in his life but the lives of his entire family.[5]

Shortly after receiving their freedom Alex and Annie

married and moved away from the Hooks Plantation, finally settling in Robertson County. As a man of some education, Alex was greatly esteemed among his own people and perceived as a leader. According to Mattie L. Grant, Alex Hooks was "a very capable preacher, influential for good." Unfortunately, that had no bearing on his family's impoverished situation.

With the Civil War and the institution of slavery not far removed, wounds were still fresh in every ex-slave's mind, body, and soul. Alex and Annie found out that freedom did not mean that life was going to be much better than it was on the plantation. During Reconstruction there was, naturally, much hostility aimed at the newly freed blacks, not to mention the animosity between the Southern and Northern whites as well. Although a regiment was stationed at nearby Cameron to keep trouble down with the Ku Klux Klan, the Freedmen's Bureau and other authorities faced much opposition. However, carpetbaggers did not wield as much power in Texas as they did in some of the other former Confederate States. Blacks were represented and politically active in the area until about 1895, serving in the state legislature and as constables and county commissioners. Hearne and Calvert were black districts in the county because of the plantations. Still the freed blacks faced dire threats and overt hatred.

Bones' Childhood

Meanwhile, Alex and Annie had eight children, five boys and three girls, with Bones being the oldest. Bones, of course, was going to become a cowboy, but his brothers and sisters were going to become schoolteachers and doctors, reflecting the influence of their parents. However, money was scarce and the only jobs available to Alex and Annie were on the plantations and the menial labor and domestic jobs that might be available in town. Some blacks were able to secure a portion of land, but not many. Needless to say, it was difficult for this family to have shelter, food on the table, clothes on their backs, and shoes on their feet. Yet Alex was a good provider and community leader, with an exceptional woman at his side. Apart from working long hours to support his family, he gave time to his community as a school-teacher and Baptist preacher. These latter activities paid little if anything at all, even in the Freedmen's Bureau, but they did set the example that Bones would emulate throughout his life and especially as a senior citizen, when he would give black youths both academic and religious instruction.

As a youth Bones didn't pay much attention to his father's preaching nor the education his father tried to give him, although he corrected those oversights as an adult. The oldest child in a house with many mouths to feed, he had to help put food on the table as soon as he became of working age. Thus, his reading and writing lessons were interrupted. As far as his religious training was concerned, he did learn to say the blessings at the supper table. Unfortunately, there was a lot more blessing than food. About all they ever had at any time in the house was "a little slab of meat, a little sugar in a paper, a jug of syrup and some flour." Then one day he was over at a white boy's house and he saw "hams hanging up, a whole barrel of sugar, a barrel of syrup," and other good things. He thought, "This is the heaven that Pa is always praying about right here." Bones promised himself he was going to have some of these good things someday and make earth a little more like heaven for himself and his friends.[6]

Bones took his first job when he was seven years old, driving a meat wagon for a butcher. At the ripe old age of nine, he was working on the Keeland Farm, where he learned to be a teamster. Still, he had chores at home and continued his often-interrupted education and religious training. As the eldest, he also had the responsibility of looking after his siblings. He was fond of saying, "They made me rock the cradle for my brothers and I've been rocking somebody's cradle ever since." The former part of the statement was certainly true, but he actually didn't rock his siblings' cradles too long. The wide-open spaces were calling, and he was listening.[7]

Undoubtedly during his childhood Bones witnessed several cattle drives passing through the county for Northern markets. It is likely he was greatly inspired by the large number of black cowboys sitting tall in the saddle on fine horses, each wearing a wide-brimmed hat, boots, spurs, a lariat, and usually a six-shooter on one side. Perhaps such an encounter as a wide-eyed youth influenced his decision to become a cowhand. Bones' birth coincided with the beginning of the cattle-industry boom, and by the time he was nine years old, trails to Northern markets were well traveled by outfits from South and West Texas. Robertson County was not as active in sending cattle up the trails, but cattle did play an important role in the county's financial progress. George Dunn, Tom Bates, and the Beals family sent a number of cattle up the trails to the markets at Dodge City and Abilene, Kansas.[8]

By 1875, when Bones was just eight years old, several black cowboys from Texas had already made names for themselves. One of the most respected was Bose Ikard of Weatherford, Texas. Bose had been a slave of Dr. Milton Ikard, who was probably his father. After being freed, he joined up with veteran cattleman Oliver Loving and then Charles Goodnight. The three of them, and others, pioneered cattle trails through badlands and hostile Indian territory. They blazed the Goodnight and Loving Trail through West Texas and New Mexico and up into Colorado. On one of their trails, Loving was killed by Comanches. After Loving's death, Bose loyally remained with Goodnight, until he returned home near Weatherford to operate his own ranch.[9]

Bones Leaves Home

These were truly times of great adventures and tales, as the whole country was enamored with the West. It was especially exciting for a youth whose imagination ran wild with stories of cowboys, cattle drives, and Indians. Bones was no different from any other boy in that he dreamed of being a cowboy. And if it was his destiny to become a cowboy of no little fame, then the beginning of that road wasn't long in coming. While he was employed on the Keeland Farm, opportunity arrived in the form of Daniel Steve Donald of the DSD Ranch, who had come to purchase feed, cattle, and a wagon with a team of oxen. As it turned out, Donald needed someone to drive the wagon and oxen back to his ranch near Lewisville in Denton County on the Red River north of Dallas. Keeland knew that young Bones was a competent teamster and suggested that Donald hire him. Alex Hooks also had the utmost confidence in his son and gave his blessing. Although Bones had never been out of the county, he was ready for some adventure. After all, he was a man according to the day's standards and had proven that he was a youth of unusual responsibility and maturity.[10]

Upon reaching the DSD Ranch, Bones remained for awhile before returning to the Keeland Farm. Donald arrived again the following summer to purchase more supplies and cattle and Bones went with the cattleman once more. This time, however, he stayed on the DSD as a full-time hand, journeying home each summer to be with his folks. Donald gave Bones a mule named Dynamite, leading Bones to declare himself "a cowboy on a mule." Thus began Bones' trail toward a cowboy life and career to which he was naturally suited.[11]

Bones worked on the DSD for four or five years, from 1877 to 1881-82. This was a tough period in Denton County, with the town of Denton being the rowdiest of all. A number of outlaws operated in the vicinity, including the likable Sam Bass, who had a Robin Hood-like reputation. Bass was shot and killed in a bank robbery in 1878. It is unknown if Bones and Bass ever crossed paths, but Bones frequented Lewisville and Denton, and he was a youth who always made acquaintances.[12]

The DSD was the first real ranch to employ Bones, but it would be far from the last. Donald took a serious liking to young Bones (which seemed to happen everywhere he went) and treated him fairly enough, and Bones was too young to know about bigotry and things relative. Yet he must have been aware of prejudice in volatile Robertson County. Perhaps all that Bones knew or wanted to know was that he was living on a ranch and living a life that beforehand he had only dreamt of.

As far as Bones was concerned, Daniel Steve Donald was honest and straightforward with him. Bones was naive and impressionable when he arrived at the DSD, but by the time he left he would know a lot about white men, and about Donald in particular. For instance, Bones had been hanging around a Durham bull breeder by the name of J. King, who was a Northerner. King had the reputation of being the best bull breeder in the area, and when a Southerner needed a bull, he went to King. Donald, Southerner that he was, didn't want Bones hanging around this "blue-belly." There was still a lot of bad feeling between Northerners and Southerners. Bones didn't understand the language Donald was using, so he took his boss's words literally. Bones recalled, "If he [Donald] told me to go after a horse with a white spot on his face I knew I'd find that kind of horse. So, I believed King had a blue belly." But on another day Bones was over at the King Ranch and saw King working with his shirt off, displaying a belly just as pale as Donald's. Bones naturally went to Donald and told him what he had found out. Donald explained that a "blue-belly" was what

Southerners called Yankees because of the color of the uniforms they had worn during the Civil War. Bones quickly learned such lessons and become a student of human character. He soon realized, "It's a good plan to investigate before you make up your mind about folks that others are calling names." This lesson and many others were secured in the back of his mind and would help form his own well-known cowboy philosophy later in life.[13]

Bones was really close to the Donald family, especially Donald's younger brother, Bob. Bones once reminisced:

> Bob and me were always cutting up together. One day Donald and all the boys ate at a restaurant in town. Bob and me were behind the rest and we ran a race to the café. I beat Bob, jumped off my horse and ran in. There were two empty seats at the counter and I took one.

But when the café man came up to Bones, he demanded to know what he was. Bones asked what he meant and the café man said, "What nationality are you?" Bones answered, "I'm Negro." That's when the café man ordered Bones out, saying, "We don't allow no niggers to eat here." The café man had a gun and reached for it. Bones jumped up and Donald told the café man to leave the youngster alone. Then he added, "I came a thousand miles to kill a so-and-so like you. Bring the boy his meal!" The café man backed down and brought a beefsteak. Bones said he didn't enjoy the beefsteak much, as it seemed to get bigger and bigger in his mouth with each chew. Afterwards, he asked Donald if he wasn't afraid the café man might shoot him. Donald said, "Naw, I knew he wouldn't shoot." Bones replied, "I wished I'd known he wouldn't. Maybe I could've enjoyed that meal."[14]

Certainly, this little bit of justice was at Bones' own peril, but it was a little justice, indeed. Apparently, there were men like Bob Donald in the Old West who stood by their men regardless of color. It is of no little wonder that Bones admired men of character such as Donald despite their other flaws. Incidents like these continued to shape Bones' unique outlook on life.

Time went by quickly and Bones was growing strong and lean. By the time he was twelve years old he was a working wrangler, feeding and taking care of the horses but not breaking or training them. That took a more experienced hand. However, he took pleasure in watching the other cowboys working the horses. He loved horses and began studying them. He noticed that a lot of the white cowboys were afraid of the meanest horses. The meanest horse on the ranch was Old Bill, whom Bones was told no one was able to ride. One Sunday morning, while the Donalds were at church and Old Bill was in the barn, Bones decided to try the outlaw horse and prove everyone wrong. He thought, "If he did throw me, he wouldn't get away with the saddle as the barn door was shut." He put the boss's saddle on him, and that went well. Then he crawled onto the saddle.

Evidently, Bones misjudged the wild horse. It broke down the barn door, tore across the lot, knocked down the stile block at the gate, and continued up the road bucking wildly, with him still in the saddle holding on for dear life. Just as the Donalds returned home from church in the buckboard, Bones somehow brought the outlaw to a halt. The astonished Donald asked, "What are you doing on that horse? He'll kill you." The boys back at the ranch were amazed, too. They asked what made him think he could ride such a horse. Bones recalled, "He [Old Bill] was made like all of the other horses and they rode them. So, I figured Old Bill could be rode, too."[15]

And he was right.

Bones also went on his first cattle drives while on the DSD. The ranch was a good-sized operation and ran a large number of cattle up the trails. Bones went on a cattle drive with Donald into what was then called Indian Territory

(Oklahoma). By then, Bones was old enough to be a real cowhand, but he was often the butt of jokes being a cowboy on a mule.

Jokes were a cowboy tradition, although some scholars have recently said that jokes were just another form of prejudice. However, ranch work and trail drives were hard occupations with little outside company for long periods, and jokes helped to break the monotony. Though Bones was the subject of lots of jokes, he learned to play jokes on other cowboys with equal cleverness. Jokes were going to be a significant outlet throughout his life, whether it was to get back at another cowhand who played a joke on him or as a way to deal with prejudice. For Bones, humor was going to break down many barriers, make lifelong friends, and open doors that were not usually open to blacks in his lifetime.

On that first trail drive into Oklahoma, the boys found an opportunity to play a good joke on Bones because he had never seen any Indians. The wars with them in this region were in the past, but some left the reservations on hunting and horse-stealing parties. The cowboys filled Bones' head with stories of Indian raiding parties and how they were able to steal a horse right out from under a man. There was a place near the river where they grazed the horses and Bones, who was in charge of them, took a nap with his mule tied to his arm. The boys discovered him while he was asleep, turned his mule loose, and let out whoops and shouts like the sound of attacking warriors. Bones jumped up and ran for his life to the stomach-gripping laughter of the cowhands. They had to cut him off before he got too far. Bones recalled years later, "I thought the Indians had me."[16]

Bones got plenty of opportunities to get back at them, and one time he played a good joke on his boss, Donald. Bones was helping him dig a well. Donald was down in the well while Bones was driving the old blind mare, Brownie, who was hauling the dirt up. Donald knew the whereabouts of the mare by the bell around its neck. Bones went into the house for something and when he returned he got the idea to take the bell off the mare's neck. He started walking toward the well while ringing the bell. Donald thought the old blind mare was walking right into the well. He started calling to Brownie, "Whoa! Whoa!" Bones recalled, "I took some dirt and threw it into the well and jingled the bell right close and Steve was sure hollering, 'Whoa, Brownie!'" Needless to say, Donald was sure worried that the old mare was going to walk right into the well and fall down on top of him.[17]

To the Wild Pecos Country

An impromptu joke played by the boys gave Bones his nickname. It all started one day when some of the hands returned from town and one brought back some dice. These dice had everything to do with his nickname and nothing to do with the fact that he was a bony and scrawny youth. Although there have been several stories, Bones personally set the story straight.

> I had never heard them called bones [the dice]. One day I happened to be around and one of the boys said, "Hand me them bones." [He misunderstood and became angry.] "My name ain't Bones!" Of course, that was as good as a bunch of cowboys wanted, to have fun. One after another was called up and it was proven that my name was Bones. I ain't never been able to get rid of that name yet.[18]

From that moment on he was never known as Mathew again, and someday the name of Bones was going to be legendary all over West Texas and the Panhandle. Bones didn't seem too upset with the nickname, for many of the cowboys had nicknames or aliases that set them apart. This name also set Bones apart. Not even a last name was needed to know who the bronc rider Bones was.

Not long after Bones got his nickname, his life took off in another direction. The DSD was running cattle on the Red River near Henrietta, Texas, in Clay County not far from Wichita Falls. Bones stayed in Henrietta awhile to tend the cattle lest they try to return from whence they came. By this time a well-traveled trail went through Henrietta, but originally the town had been slow to develop due to Indian hostilities, particularly the Comanches, and the Civil War, which had left settlers unprotected. Most left the area during the war, but deserters and desperados stayed until the end of the war. Later, ranchers grazed cattle in the area but continued to be harassed by various Indian tribes who were trying to remain on their land. Settlement eventually began about 1869, when Henry A. Whaley set up a colony, but the 1870s still saw some attacks. In spite of this, a buffalo hunters' supply center was established and a cattle trail went through Henrietta. More settlers arrived between 1875 and 1879, and by 1880 the Indian troubles appeared to be over and the county became the judicial center for the Panhandle. The Fort Worth & Denver Railroad laid tracks through Henrietta in 1882, headed for the Panhandle, and certain things in the name of progress were inevitable.[19]

Bones may have been in Henrietta when the railroad went through. He had certainly been in Gainesville in neighboring Cooke County the previous year. At the time Donald left him in Henrietta, it was considered serious cattle country. Many outfits drove cattle through Henrietta and some were from the West Texas frontier. Bones noticed one of those outfits one day as it came across the plains with a wagon and remuda (several horses). Bones got on his mule and rode out to meet them to find out who they were and where they were going. He was a curious youth who seemed never to meet a stranger and turned most into friends. The outfit, he learned, was run by J. R. Norris of the JRE Ranch in the Pecos country, a wild and untamed region.

The JRE cowboys had a few inquiries of their own and wanted to know if the slender, black youth on a mule was a real cowhand. Bones proudly said that he was and they laughed at him, insinuating no cowboy rode a mule. Bones angered, but had grit. He quickly challenged their best rider to a horse race. They eagerly accepted and confidently let Bones choose one of their horses out of the remuda. They did not realize that, though young, he was an excellent judge of horse flesh. To their humiliation, he beat their best rider with one of their own horses.[20]

J. R. Norris had been watching the proceedings with interest. He was a pretty good judge of character and was impressed with the scrawny youth. Norris offered Bones a deal. He promised a new pair of boots and five horses in exchange for the mule and promised to make him into a real cowboy if he joined the outfit. Bones immediately took Norris up on his offer, parted company with his mule, and rode out of Henrietta with the Pecos outfit. Not surprisingly, Bones did not ride any more mules after that.[21]

Bones' decision that day was based on trust in the man, J. R. Norris, according to his first impression. Traveling with strangers to parts unknown was a gamble, indeed. Bones was fortunate. Sometimes youths, especially blacks, were tricked or forced to go on cattle drives. More often than not, these orphans were usually the ones chosen to test swollen waters or a dangerous, shaky swinging bridge over a river or canyon. A number of stories illustrate this danger and one in particular, that of Birl Brown, a contemporary of Bones, magnifies Bones' good judgment about J. R. Norris.

Birl Brown lived in a rented house on the outskirts of Tyler, Texas, with his mother, who was employed by the owner of the house. One day, as a result of youthful curiosity,

Birl followed a cattle-herding outfit and got too far from home. Suddenly, a rider came up and offered Birl a ride, which he accepted. He was placed in a wagon driven by the outfit's cook, a black man named Boze, and the cook was ordered to guard the kid well. Unknown to Birl, this was no ride but a kidnapping. When Birl realized the situation, the cook poured whiskey down his throat to sedate him. He awoke hours later after the outfit had long been on the trail. The boy never saw home again and ended up in Clarendon in the Panhandle, where he spent the rest of his life.[22]

Bones' situation on the trail was not at all similar to that of Birl. J. R. Norris did not kidnap Bones, but promised him a job and kept that promise by treating him like a real cowhand with real cowhand wages. In the Pecos country, Bones honed his skills and became a great bronc rider whose reputation spread far and wide. Also here, Bones grew into a man of strong character, not forgetting the instructions and influence of his father, the teacher and Baptist preacher.

CHAPTER 2

The Pecos and the Panhandle: The Pioneer Years

In the pioneer days there wasn't much race feeling. . . .
When a man rode up to a door, no one looked at his color.
—Bones Hooks

When they reached the Pecos country, Bones was
impressed because "this was real cattle country." There was
no law west of the Pecos River, despite the popular saying.
Not even the infamous Judge Roy Bean's long arm, which
meted out his own special brand of justice, reached into the
Pecos country around the Davis Mountains, as he would
have many believe. Bones remarked, "Folks talk about Judge
Bean and the law west of the Pecos, but there was no law out
there then."[1] It was a wild, rugged country, where the only
real law was the Colt and Winchester.

The Pecos country in West Texas and Eastern New
Mexico was more than real cattle country; it was a haven for
outlaws. With the absence of true law and order, the ranchers and leading citizens took the law into their own hands by
forming organized mobs called vigilantes. These men were
judge, jury, and hangman all rolled into one. There were
usually no appeals and little mercy. Not only did they round
up the hated cattle rustlers, but killers and rapists, also.

There was little civilization, law, and authority, except Fort Stockton and Fort Davis south of the Davis Mountains, Fort Bliss near the Mexico border, and Fort Stanton to the north in New Mexico, all of which were days' rides away. The first town site in the area was Toyah in Pecos County, which was started as a trading post in 1880-81 and then the Texas & Pacific Railroad laid out a town site as a shipping point. The Texas & Pacific also proposed to build a depot on the western side of the Pecos River. This site became the Pecos Station and later the town of Pecos. Prior to this, however, a camp for cattle drives had been established on the eastern side of the river before moving to the west bank where the town was platted. By 1883-84, Reeves County was created out of Pecos County, and Pecos City, platted in 1885, was named the county seat. As many as twenty-four town sites were applied for in Reeves County, but only a handful exist today.[2]

In the Davis Mountains region, Bones earned his reputation as a great bronc rider and horse trainer. He participated in roundups, cattle drives, and all aspects of ranch life, but it was his bronc-riding ability and horse-training skills that set him apart and that were in such great demand.

Bones was never an all-around cowboy or top hand such as the amazing Jim Perry of the XIT Ranch. He had no ambitions to herd cattle, be a wagon boss, or command an outfit as did Pecos contemporary Addison Jones. No, Bones was a specialist. He went wherever there were horses to break, and he always had spectators. Boys would watch him ply his trade as they stood on or straddled a section of corral fence. Bones would crawl into the saddle and the wild ride would begin, the horse flailing and snorting as it tried to throw its rider to the ground. It didn't happen much. But when it did, he'd remember what the horse did to throw him, dust off his rawhide, put his hat back on, which was a derby in those days, and get back on and try it again.

Some have suggested that Bones was a horse whisperer,

but according to his own testimony, he was not. A horse whisperer was a rare breed, indeed, and most cowhands had never met one nor seen one in action. Certainly, there were different methods of breaking a wild horse. Some did it in water, while others shackled the ankles, which took a chance of permanently hobbling the animal. But the majority of horse breakers used the old-fashioned way, with dirt and sweat and, quite often, blood. Someone once asked Bones his method and he said that he just got on and rode. He didn't use any fancy methods or tricks. However, he was being modest when he said he just got on and rode, for he was a student of the art of bronc riding and studied horses as much as he studied the character of men. He'd watch the other cowboys ride, and while the boys were whooping and hollering, he'd be sizing up the wild horse. He said it usually took several rides before a horse was really tamed. Some horses gave in after just a few bucks, but Bones admitted that some were never ridden by anyone, not even him.[3]

Bones was such an accomplished rider that he knew which way a horse would jump or buck. He said there were four ways a horse would jump or buck and he knew precisely what to do to make a horse jump or buck a certain way. Bones proved time and time again that he was an exceptional rider, and when the Pecos boys finally realized that he was one of the best bronc riders in that country, they quit bringing him wild horses just to see if he'd get thrown. Instead, they brought him horses to break and train.[4]

Bones was not afraid of mean horses. Personally, he liked to ride the meanest ones. His toughness was measured by his never refusing to ride any horse. This won him respect and friendship with whites in the region. At the age of sixteen, he was already a top bronc rider, and by the time he was nineteen, his name was known all over the Pecos country.

Wherever Bones worked, he was almost exclusively in charge of the remuda. He rarely worked cattle. When he went on cattle drives, it was as wrangler. Sometimes he drove herds of horses to market or various ranches. The cattle markets in Kansas were far from the Pecos country. There were other markets in Louisiana and California, but the Kansas markets were the destinations of the Pecos outfits. During the trail drives, Bones' job was to care for the horses and provide fresh mounts to the trail hands. Undoubtedly, the drives were long and hard. West Texas was isolated from the main cattle trails, so they had to carve out their own. On these trail drives from the Pecos to the Kansas markets, Bones first saw the flat, treeless prairie lands of the Texas Panhandle. It was there he would make his final home and lasting legacy.

He made his first trail drives to Abilene and Kiowa, Kansas, with J. R. Norris's JRE outfit. They left between March and May and the route they took strategically missed the Pease, Brazos, and Colorado rivers by crossing them at their heads. This took them through Midland, Shafter near Lubbock (this Shafter no longer exists, although another is located in Presidio County), and the Yellow House Canyon. Then they entered the Panhandle and struck the once-inaccessible Palo Duro Canyon and towards present-day Amarillo. They took advantage of the full lakes, such as the one at Amarillo named Wild Horse Lake. This lake had been known by the Comanches and other tribes long before the white man or the comancheros discovered it. While they watered the herd at Wild Horse Lake, Bones liked to go to higher ground just north of this site, where he was able to see the Plains for miles and miles. Years later he would establish a "Negro Addition" or town in this very same place. From Wild Horse Lake they traveled northeast, crossed the Canadian River towards Lipscomb County, entered the Oklahoma Panhandle, and reached Kiowa, just across the Kansas line. The round trip took seven to eight months, arriving at the markets by September and returning home, hopefully, by Christmas.[5]

Bones was just one of the numerous cowboys making the trail drives to Kansas from various originations. Black cowboys made up about one in four on the trail drives, while Mexican vaqueros were about two in five. Blacks undoubtedly had larger numbers on the trails than on the home ranch. The big operations often hired professional trail drivers like Ab Blocker of Tom Green County, Texas, who brought the first cattle to the 3,000,000-acre XIT Ranch. These trail drivers were young and wild and so were their men. They were real cow*boys*, in that most ranged from mere boys to those in their early twenties. They were also culturally diverse, being white, Mexican, black, and Indian. An older trusted hand might go along to make sure the cattle arrived at their destination and nothing unusual occurred. Mature blacks also went on the long trail drives because it was an insufferable job and many whites wanted no part of it year in and year out. Most whites participated in only a few trail drives before they gave it up, which is why professional trail drivers were in top demand. Perhaps as many as 40 percent of the trail hands were black, while the year-round ranch hands were a much higher ratio of whites.[6]

Trail Drives

Bones went on his share of trail drives, but not with the professional trail drivers. Most of the outfits that employed him were smaller operations like J. R. Norris's JRE, which handled their own trail drives. As the ranch's wrangler, he was expected to go. But a trail drive was also a means to get from one place to another and get paid for it, and wherever he ended up there was much demand for his expertise.

While Bones was making the most of these trail drives from the Pecos region, Amarillo was not even in existence. There were just three towns in the Panhandle's twenty-six counties during the early 1880s, and most of the land was divided up among large cattle operations, a number of which had foreign owners or investors. Like the Pecos, it was real cattle country. The prairie land that Easterners thought was the Great American Desert was actually perfect grazing land, with grass that was belly high to a horse and rarely another settler within a hundred miles.

Still, the Panhandle was no easy place to live in those days. This region was subjected to devastating blizzards that swept down out of the north, continually strong winds, tornadoes, droughts, dust storms, outlaws, and an abundance of rattlesnakes and lobos, otherwise known as wolves, who were great predators of cattle. Often in these wide-open spaces, it was difficult to tell the time, and the legendary cattleman Charles Goodnight did not take this uncertainty casually, especially on a cattle drive. He preferred to entrust the keeping of time to one of his black cowboys. He believed that blacks had the uncanny ability of always knowing the day and time, whether it was day or night. In fact, many cowhands were very adept at keeping time and few ever owned a timepiece. Of course, the sun was a dependable timekeeper most days, as the West Texas and Panhandle skies were often clear and bright. At night it was necessary to know the hour during the night watch, and the cook had to know when it was time to start the coffee and breakfast while most of the hands were still asleep. They learned to read the sun, moon, and stars with great skill. Probably the most important navigation tool was the Big Dipper in relation to the North Star, which guided them as it had others many centuries before.

Bones' perspective on the trail was interesting, to say the least. He once said, "Lord, I don't know what years them was. I just knowed daylight and dark."[7] This does not suggest that Goodnight's faith in the black cowhands was misplaced. It simply means that Bones' recollection of those times was different and that he never mastered the art of reading the stars.

But certain things were a given on the trails. Seldom was there any company other than themselves. Contrary to what popular fiction would have you believe, there was not a lot of activity outside of working, eating, and sleeping. They had to get along with each other for months at a time. Maybe someone had a harmonica. They sang old songs or made up new ones and played jokes to break the boredom, but truthfully there was a lot of loneliness and depression. There was a lot of rugged, unsettled land between the Pecos region and the Kansas markets, and much of it was open range that appeared endless on the horizon. By 1883, barbed wire had barely begun to crop up on the vast Panhandle lands that Bones traveled across. Bones said a "white man" was seldom on these trails, "maybe one a day, some line rider or fence rider," where there was a fence or perhaps one going up.[8]

When they arrived in Abilene or Kiowa there were numerous black cowboys from various outfits, and more arrived daily during the market season. Some outfits were entirely black or Mexican; others were white or mixed. The saloons, dancehalls, and gambling houses catered to blacks and there were even black saloon girls and prostitutes, although the proprietors of the red-light businesses probably enforced segregation. Black cowboys had much freedom in these towns as they roamed the streets, frequented the saloons, bought whiskey and women, and sometimes caused trouble and ended up in jail just like their white counterparts. As noted earlier, such events were largely written out of history by white writers until recent decades.

When Bones returned to the Pecos country, he was a minority again. A considerable number of blacks worked the Davis Mountain range ranches, but they were isolated from each other and rarely seen in town. Still, some were widely known. Other than Bones there were 7D George Adams, George McJunkin, and Addison Jones, more commonly known as Nigger Ad. Just about all of the black cowboys were referred to as "Nigger" something. While it is difficult not to consider the word derogatory, several white cowboys claimed to intend no insult by it. With the Civil War not many years in the past, one must wonder how the terms "Yankee" and "Rebel" might compare in that era.[9]

Bones' contemporary, Ad Jones, was several years older than Bones and had been born a slave. Their paths must have crossed in the fall and spring roundups. However, Bones never mentioned Ad in the material he left behind nor his many interviews. But Bones did not mention a lot of black cowboys. He was more interested in telling of cowboy experiences without mentioning the color of one's skin. But Ad was well known up and down the Pecos from Toyah, Texas, to Las Vegas, New Mexico, and was widely considered one of the best cowhands in the Pecos region. During his long career he worked mostly for George W. Littlefield of the LFD Ranch. He had that man's undying respect, and offered his loyalty in return.[10]

The Return Home

7D George and Ad found lifelong homes on specific ranches where they were usually respected and treated fairly. Bones on the other hand was never a longtime employee of any particular ranch, but he worked at one time or another for most of the ranches in the Pecos region. As a horse breaker and trainer, he went wherever there were wild horses to break and train. Instead of taking a monthly salary with room and board, he preferred to get paid for every horse he broke, for he could break many in a season. There was always work for a man such as Bones, so he never went without work very long.

His trade allowed him to profit, and it didn't hurt that he

was quite thrifty. By the time he was nineteen years old he had accumulated a herd of cattle and horses under the B Brand. In the pioneer years, a cowhand could still brand mavericks on the open range, collect a herd, and graze it on the ranch lands where he worked. A cowhand could better himself this way. The foreign-owned ranches and large operations would end that practice by the late 1880s.

Then Bones became homesick. He had been in the Pecos for about five years and had grown into a man. He desired to return home to Northeast Texas and visit his folks. So, he sold his horses and cattle to finance his journey and went back with money in his pocket.

After a reunion with his parents and brothers and sisters, he decided to stay in that part of the country. For five years he had been saving money. He didn't drink, smoke, spend it on wild women, or gamble it away in the cow towns, and he had put away a considerable sum for such a time. Strangely, he ended up at Wamba in Bowie County near Texarkana. This was not far from the old Hooks Plantation, where Bones' parents had been slaves. He purchased a store and for the next eighteen months made his home there as a respectable, but young, businessman. One day he arrived at his store to find this sign posted:

We Give You Thirty-Six Hours
To Get Out.
White Caps of Sand Gall Gizzard[11]

It took him about three hours to vacate the premises and he never went back. He had enough of the white man's hospitality in Northeast Texas. Maybe he remembered why he was willing to leave that part of the country in the first place. After he left Wamba he returned to Denton County and, more than likely, visited his old home ranch, the DSD near Lewisville. He also visited Dallas and Henrietta and went up to Clarendon. He liked what he saw in Clarendon.

By this time, barbed wire was changing the landscape that Bones had first seen and admired in the early 1880s. Many of the ranches were now fenced off and the nesters (home-steaders) fenced in, which often cut them off from main roads and the water supply. Before the fencing, the cattle might drift hundreds of miles during the winter, but not so during the winter of 1886-87. Thousands of cattle froze to death, piled on top of each other at the fences. Bones spent part of that winter in Henrietta and part in the Panhandle. He said, "You could have put dead cows three feet apart and had enough to reach Colorado." That winter crippled many of the ranches and some were never able to recover. Some of the smaller outfits were entirely wiped out.[12]

Bones went up to Mobeetie in the northeastern part of the Panhandle following the devastating winter. Mobeetie, the first town established in the Panhandle in 1876, was still wild. It grew up alongside Fort Elliott, which had been the Panhandle's only frontier fort, created after the end of the Red River (Indian) War of 1874-75, in which the U.S. made war against the Federation of Comanches, Kiowas, and Cheyenne during our country's ruthless expansionist move-ment. Mobeetie had originally been a buffalo hunters' sup-ply camp, then became known as Sweetwater and finally Mobeetie, reportedly a Comanche word that means sweet water or soft water. In its short history it was visited by such personalities as Bat Masterson, Buffalo Bill, Temple Houston, and the notorious outlaw Crawford Goldsby of Cherokee and black descent, whose alias was Cherokee Bill. It was in Mobeetie that Bat Masterson was wounded, result-ing in a limp that required the use of a cane for the rest of his life. This, of course, added to his mystique when he later became a lawman.

Bones didn't like Mobeetie much and he had good rea-son. Apart from being a rowdy town, it had a reputation of being unfriendly towards blacks and he didn't stay long. But about the time that Bones was there, a sensational trial was going on. Sgt. Charles Connors of the all-black Twenty-Fourth Infantry was on trial for murdering a black soldier. Sergeant Connors had been transporting prisoners to Fort Leavenworth when the train he was on was held up. Instead of shooting it out with the bandits and risking the passengers' lives, he turned over his gun at the conductor's request. The train was robbed and he continued on to Fort Leavenworth with his prisoners. Upon his return to Fort Elliott, those in his own outfit were angry that he didn't fight it out and many called him a coward. One private threatened Connors' life with a gun. The sergeant reacted and killed the private in what he claimed was self-defense. He was court-martialed by the army and then turned over to the civilian court in Mobeetie, where he was found guilty and sentenced to prison. Apparently, his military superiors overlooked his nineteen years of good service and spotless record, and the courts at Mobeetie were equally merciless. However, his former superiors came forth a few years later and he was eventually pardoned, but only after the damage was already done.

Despite Mobeetie's reputation, most blacks who lived in the Panhandle prior to 1890 lived there, and a number worked at Fort Elliott or made their living off it. A smaller number was employed on the surrounding ranches. The federal census did not include the black soldiers stationed at Fort Elliott, specifically the Tenth Cavalry, better known as Buffalo Soldiers, and also the Twenty-Fourth Infantry. They served the fort and the Panhandle from 1879 to 1887, and between 1881 and 1887 all of the enlisted soldiers at the fort were black troopers. They were frequently the only protection the settlers had from outlaws and occasional raiding parties from the reservations. Along with the Texas Rangers and the local sheriffs, these soldiers were responsible for enforcing law and order throughout the Panhandle.[13]

The Panhandle

Bones returned to Clarendon, which he had visited during the winter of 1886-87. He found the town immensely to his liking. Clarendon was the third town established in the Panhandle (1878), after Mobeetie and Tascosa. Rev. Lewis H. Carhart, a Methodist minister, founded this Christian colony. The local cowboys called Clarendon "Saints Roost" because of its religious atmosphere. The Methodists operated the colony with strictness, keeping saloons and gambling houses outside of the city limits, although reportedly a respectable citizen kept a secret supply of good liquor for his important clientele.The Methodists even tried to require that anyone settling in the town be Methodist, but it was too difficult to enforce.

Pastor Carhart actually did not preach frequently in Clarendon. He mostly divided his time between promoting the colony and pursuing his real-estate venture, the Quarter Circle Heart Ranch and the Clarendon Land and Investment Company, which was in part owned by British stockholders. While Carhart was away in locations such as New York and London, leading citizens held together the colony, in particular, his brother-in-law Judge Benjamin Horton White, who has been recognized as the "Father of Donley County." He was the county's first judge when it was organized in 1882.[14]

The Methodists' control was further aided by John Rosenthal, affectionately known as "Rosie," who was Judge White's business partner. He was Jewish, however. The real backbone of the colony was the many devout Christians—several retired ministers and the powerful ranchers and their wives, the most influential rancher being Charles Goodnight.

Goodnight was arguably the first rancher in the Panhandle, establishing the JA Ranch with financier John

Adair of Ireland. Goodnight was a man of law and order, even if he sometimes took the law into his own hands. He enforced strict rules on his ranch, forbidding gambling and liquor. The Methodists were fortunate to have such an ally, but perhaps their staunchest ally was Goodnight's wife, Mary ("Molly") Ann Dyer. She was an extremely strong woman who had spent many months alone when her husband was busy establishing the JA. Other times, she went on cattle drives without any special treatment. However, she was a woman of culture and desperately wanted schools, churches, and civilization to come to the Panhandle.

While significant civilization did not arrive in the Panhandle until the railroads built lines from one end to the other, citizens of Clarendon were not without culture. Many were educated at the best universities in the East, and others were accustomed to having household servants, which some did employ on the frontier. The citizens brought a remnant of their culture with them in the form of large and expensive pianos, although the first homes were really not large enough to accommodate such a luxury.

The Fort Worth & Denver Railroad arrived at Clarendon in 1887, about the same time Bones was breaking horses for Charles Goodnight at the JA, but the railroad bypassed Clarendon approximately five and a half miles to the south. In the absence of Carhart, who couldn't have made it back in time anyway, town citizens met with railroad officials and agreed to move the town so they could be on the railroad route. It was too late by the time Carhart arrived, and the colony would be forever changed. Outsiders became part of the citizenry and saloons were some of the new businesses, but the Christian element remained strong and the saloon owners went out of their way not to make enemies of the Methodists. Eventually, the Christians voted Prohibition in and liquor and gambling out. Clarendon retained its "Saints Roost" reputation despite the presence of secular residents and secular ways. Churches were quickly established in New Clarendon, which strangely had not been truly established in the old colony, and the new town became the religious and educational center of the Panhandle.[15]

Bones liked Clarendon a lot and he said that he broke horses for most of the ranches in the area, which seems accurate. Therefore he knew most of the black cowboys. Some whom he undoubtedly knew were Burns Clark, Gus Hartman, Arthur Goodwin, and Purvis, all whom were employed by Carhart's Quarter Circle Heart Ranch. There were others in the region as well, most notably Billy Freeman, and there was Birl Brown of the Koogle Ranch, Samuel Montgomery, and George Armstead of the LX Ranch or the Frying Pan Ranch. Near Mobeetie there was a bronc buster named George Washington. In Collingsworth, Childress, and Hall counties in the southeastern Panhandle, on the Diamond Tail owned by Bill Curtis, there were several cowhands and cooks. Not the least of the Panhandle cowboys was the famed Jim Perry of the XIT Ranch, which covered parts of nine counties. However, cowboys and outfit cooks were not the only blacks in the region. A number were domestics, such as Martha, Goodnight's housekeeper. She had three children who grew up in the Goodnight home, Hattie, Maud, and Tom. Of course, there were many others whose names have been forgotten and lost.[16]

Bones and the Goodnights

When Bones worked for Goodnight, he was always the top wrangler for that irascible man. They were like two bulls banging into one another, grunting, snorting, and slobbering. Goodnight was the older bull, of course, already established and legendary. Bones was the young bull but quickly making a name for himself.

Goodnight was considered the heartbeat of the Panhandle by many. The entire region looked to him for guidance and felt that the direction of the Panhandle lay squarely on his shoulders. Goodnight was about fifty years old when Bones first went to work for him in 1887. He was a hardened cattle baron who ran roughshod over others, cursed with the best of them, and had little mercy on those who opposed him. Yet most of his cowhands who thought he was a hard man also considered him fair minded. He hated lazy cowboys and would test them with menial jobs just to see if they really wanted to work or just to eat off the chuck wagon. Bones liked working for Goodnight because the man had one quality that Bones appreciated and admired. He had no qualms about hiring black cowboys and treated them about the same as the others. Goodnight's association with black cowboys went back more than twenty years to when he and Oliver Loving had been partners.

During the late 1860s, one black cowboy became the example to Goodnight of what a cowboy should be. He was Bose Ikard. They were friends and "brothers" as far as the times and racial barriers allowed. Ikard "was probably the most devoted man to me I ever had," Goodnight remarked. "I trusted him farther than any living man. He was my detective, banker and everything else in Colorado, New Mexico and all the other wild country I was in . . . and was the most skilled and trustworthy man I had."[17]

Bones likewise respected Goodnight more than any other man he had known. Goodnight, at times, appeared larger than the Panhandle. He awed some of his contemporaries and spawned hate in others. Bones understood that it took men like Goodnight to help bring civilization to the frontier. That had not been the cattle barons' original purpose, but these powerful men did clear the way. Bones realized the historical importance of Goodnight and those who were to follow in his footsteps. Yet he wasn't blinded by his respect for

Charles Goodnight, about fifty years of age. *Courtesy of the Panhandle-Plains Historical Museum, Canyon, Tex.*

the man, for he said that Goodnight was a "queer old man." That opinion was the result of a wild horse Bones had broken and trained. He indicated that he had trained that horse better than any horse he had ever trained and taught it to perform many tricks. As he expected praise, he called Goodnight out of the house to see the horse. After the horse performed tricks and stunts, Goodnight said, "Hmmmph. If you were smarter, the horse would be smarter." And he went back inside the house without another word.[18]

Bones' feelings were hurt. He was in a bad way and needed some encouragement at that particular time. The cowman was tough on Bones and never told him what a great hand he was with horses. He never complimented his best bronc buster and wrangler that way. Yet he frequently bragged about Bones' amazing skills to his rancher friends. Years later, at one of the cowboy reunions, Bones asked Goodnight why he never said anything good about his abilities. Goodnight told Bones he didn't want his best hand to quit.

Bones was right. Goodnight was as peculiar as his reply. But the circumstance did not alter Bones' admiration for the controversial cowman. Many years later, when Bones was the leader of the black community in the region, contemporaries wanted to erect a monument in Bones' honor. Bones gave his blessing but insisted that Goodnight's name be engraved on the cornerstone.[19] The monument was not completed, but another was constructed and dedicated almost thirty years after his death.

As much as Bones respected Goodnight, he respected his wife, Molly Ann, even more. He always had a soft spot in his heart for the pioneer women—the hardships and loneliness they went through—and he felt that they never received their due respect and honor.

Molly Ann Dyer was from Tennessee and came from a family of some renown. Her grandfather was Henry Robert Dyer, who figured prominently in the Battle of New Orleans in the War of 1812 under "Old Hickory," Gen. Andrew Jackson. Her father, Joel Henry Dyer, was the attorney general of the West District of Tennessee. When Molly Ann became Mrs. Goodnight, she was much more than a wife. She was a housekeeper, a cook, and sometimes a companion on the trail drives. She also handled all of the correspondence and book-keeping, as her husband was illiterate. She was fondly called "the mother of the Panhandle," as she was the first white woman to settle in the region. But the term more appropriate-ly reflected the affection of the cowboys—or her "boys," as she called all of them. She never had any children of her own, but Bones said she treated the cowboys like her sons:

> She was like a mother to all of the cowboys. She'd say, "When have you wrote your mother?" All the cowboys just worshiped her.[20]

Being a strong advocate of church and school, Molly Ann later established the Goodnight College in Goodnight, Texas. She was also influential in many other civic affairs. She wanted more than cattle on the ranch and may have been one of the first to envision the Plains' conversion from cattle to crop farming. She planted crops and was responsible for saving the buffalo, whose offspring survive in the Panhandle today.

Bones' skill as a bronc rider was always in top demand, so he did not remain with the Goodnights for long. Unlike the jobs of other ranch hands, his job lasted only as long as there were wild horses to break and train, which took him to numerous outfits. The pay was twenty-five dollars a month with room and board or three dollars a head, and he usually took the latter.

Almost Hanged

Not long after he had arrived in the Panhandle, Bones hired himself out to a small outfit that was rustling cattle. He was unaware of this. One day vigilantes stormed into their camp and gave the rustlers a speedy trial, including Bones. They hanged two men and were going to hang Bones, too, but "Skillety Bill" Johnson of the Frying Pan Ranch, with whom Bones had become friends, intervened. Skillety Bill told his brother vigilantes that Bones wasn't a rustler, that he didn't know what was going on, that he was too young to know about this kind of stuff. Skillety Bill must have been quite convincing because they did something rare. They agreed to let Bones go. Then Skillety Bill proved his mettle and friendship further. He took Bones to aside and advised him to get out of the region for awhile until things cooled down. Bones had just arrived in the Panhandle a short time ago and liked it. But he was no fool. He took his friend's advice, and he learned another lesson about character that he hid in his heart. He found out that day that no matter how mean a mob might get, "there's always one man who was willing to stand up for what was right." That one courageous man saved Bones, and Bones adopted that principle in his own life.[21]

Bones temporarily left the Panhandle and worked in Southern Colorado, Western Oklahoma, Eastern New Mexico, and Henrietta, Texas, but no place seemed like home more than the wide open spaces of the Panhandle. He felt that was where he belonged and where he must someday return. But if he left the Panhandle to escape possible trouble, he was going to find a different kind of trouble in some of the places he was going.

Bones was taking some TXT horses to Forth Worth, across "No Man's Land" in what is now Greer County in Western Oklahoma. As they were crossing a swinging bridge, Bones' pack horse was knocked into the water, soaking Bones' gear and bedroll. Later that night he rode up to a house and shouted. When a man came to the door, Bones asked for bedding and hay for his horse. The man hospitably obliged.

Bones found hay in the barn where the man said it would be, but no bedding. He returned to the house and called out for that bedding again. To his surprise the man told Bones to sleep in the guestroom, which was usually reserved for preachers and ranchers. Bones recalled, "I never went to bed feeling so good to wake up feeling so bad because a little girl was peeking through the curtain on the door and I heard her say, 'Mama, I believe there's a nigger in there.' The mother looked in and said, 'I know it is.'"

Bones knew what that meant and who were his hosts. He dressed as quickly as he could and was still putting on his clothes on his way out to the barn. He saddled his horse and was just about to ride out when the man of the house appeared and demanded to know what Bones was doing sleeping in his bed. Bones answered, "You told me to."

"Yeah, but you're a nigger," the man replied.

Bones told the man that he had never been able to change that. Then the man said, "Ain't many of you in this country."

Bones didn't plan on being there much longer, either. Because Bones was black, the man charged him for the hay and the night's sleep, which came to $7.50. Bones felt he was fortunate to get away that easily in a strange land with no friends. Still, one would have to wonder why the man didn't know Bones was black. Perhaps it was because of the darkness and his skin was covered with trail dust. And it may have been his language. The cowboys had their own lingo and Bones probably talked like all the other cowboys.[22]

Bones eventually returned to Clarendon after a season or so and found work right away. The rustling incident seemed to have been forgotten. Then he returned to the Pecos region. His work was always going to take him back and forth from the Panhandle to the Pecos country because he liked the Pecos almost as well as the Panhandle. Besides working for the JRE in the Pecos, he broke horses for Perry Autman, who owned a large horse ranch; George Brookshire, of the big Hashknife Ranch; Bill Ross, who bought a remnant of the old Hashknife; the Chicago C; and the Cowan Ranch, but it was T. J. McIlroy of the TJM for whom he broke the most horses. In the Panhandle his work was just as much in demand. There were the JA and the Goodnight Ranch, the Herald R. R., the Christian Brothers, the LX, J. D. Jefferies, the White Deer, the RO, and a number of small outfits. Bones was now recognized as the best bronc rider and horse trainer from the Pecos to the Panhandle.[23]

Meanwhile, a new town had been established in the Central Panhandle. It was Amarillo, in Potter County, and it soon became the largest rural shipping center in the country as well as the most important town on the High Plains, due to the coming of the railroad across this vast region. By the late 1880s the trails were rarely traveled to distant markets in Kansas. Now cattle were usually driven to the nearest rail-shipping point, which meant Amarillo for much of the Texas Panhandle. They were herded into railcars and transported to markets. However, some smaller outfits still made the long trail drive, as they could not afford railcar transport.

Amarillo's establishment as a railroad town was not unique. Most of the county seats in the Panhandle developed because of the railroad route. The town began when the Irish railroad workers set up a tent city called "Ragtown" at the end of the line. It grew to approximately five hundred, as opportunists, town-site men, merchants, saloon men, and land promoters joined them. A railroad depot was secured and an election for the county seat followed. It was a wild town at first. The sheriff of Tascosa, in neighboring Oldham County, who had jurisdiction over the new town, hired a young LX cowboy, James Gober, to be the temporary law. After Amarillo was incorporated, he became the town's first sheriff. He later was ousted on an indictment for murder, although he was acquitted.[24]

Bones didn't like Amarillo in its early days because of its rampant lawlessness. Another town he didn't like was Tascosa, so he spent very little time there. Tascosa was the wildest town in the Panhandle in the 1880s and possibly the wildest in the West. It had been established in 1878 as a supply point for the ranchers, but it catered to the cowboys with an unending supply of liquor, gambling, and women—not necessarily in that order. Many of those who had been run out of Mobeetie found a home in Tascosa. Even the infamous Billy the Kid was welcomed in Tascosa.

The mid-1880s proved to be a troublesome time for the young town, and two incidents that nearly destroyed it spread its reputation of being wild and lawless. The first event was a cowboy strike, resulting partly from many ranches being run by absentee owners and foreign investors. The cowboys demanded increased wages, but it was also far more complicated than that. (See John L. McCarty's *Maverick Town: The Story of Old Tascosa*.) Tom Harris, an LS wagon boss, was the leader of the spring 1883 strike. The large ranches banded together and defeated the hundred or so strikers, and most of the participants were blacklisted from working Panhandle ranches, particularly Harris. Following the strike, rustling became a serious problem and much of it was blamed on Harris's cattle syndicate. The syndicate was a cooperation of small ranchers and nesters who organized in order to compete with the large ranches such as the XIT, LX, and LS.

Tom Harris's syndicate became enough of a threat that the LS Ranch hired Pat Garrett, the killer of Billy the Kid, as a special Texas Ranger to break up the rustling, but many believed the real purpose was to destroy the syndicate. Garrett set up headquarters at the LS Ranch and spent a year on the job. His success was nominal, but he did break up the Gatlin Gang. After Garrett left, some of the hands at the LS who had been Garrett's Home Rangers continued the war with the Harris faction. Townspeople took sides, and in the spring of 1886, deadly violence exploded in a cowboy fight between Harris's men and the LS hands, which left three dead, others seriously wounded, and numerous questions unanswered. Needless to say, the battle at Tascosa's Boot Hill became as famous—or infamous—as the one at Tombstone. Yet these incidents did not kill Tascosa. That happened when the railroad bypassed Tascosa and "Ragtown" was established, which became Amarillo. Tascosa slowly disappeared into history until it no longer existed, except in memories.[25]

Back in the Pecos

Meanwhile, Bones was back in the Pecos breaking horses for Perry Autman and the Cowan Ranch in late 1887 and early 1888. His best friend was a young white cowboy named Tommy Monroe Clayton. They were real friends and partners in the truest sense of the words. Bones broke and trained horses while his friend took care of the business of selling them. Bones remembered: "We made a good team because Tommy wasn't awfully strong physically, but he was sure smart. He had the mental and I had the physical."[26]

Bones and Tommy went around a lot together. They went hunting, fishing, and camping, and they especially loved watching horse races. When you saw one of these cowboys, you saw the other. That was how close they were. They went all over the countryside together. They were about as close as two friends could get, and they equally shared the money from their horse business. Their lives were interwoven, and Clayton would play an important role in Bones' future, even if indirectly.

Their friendship reveals something about the pioneer times that is often overlooked. There was little of society's prejudice to keep them apart, despite the difference of race. But as the railroads brought more people and civilization,

they would find out that, even out on the frontier, a friendship between a black and a white could only go so far.
Something would change their relationship forever, and I
will cover it in the next chapter.

Late in the decade, Bones was back in Clarendon, breaking many more wild horses. About 1890 he was in Ennis,
Texas, on business. His future wife lived here, but she was
just nine years old at this time. Needless to say, romance did
not bring him to Ennis. However, there was a man there
named W. H. (Wiley Holder) Fuqua. They became friends
and Fuqua would help Bones in the years to come. Perhaps
it was Bones who suggested that Fuqua go to Amarillo, as
there were a lot of opportunities for a man of Fuqua's talents. That's what Fuqua did. He had successfully operated a
school in Ennis but also accumulated over twenty thousand
dollars on the side in the cattle business. He detested poli-
tics, but the people of Ennis tried to run him for public
office. It was then that he and his wife left for a new destination and ended up in Amarillo permanently. Fuqua did not
look for another school position, but invested in a ranch
and also purchased a livery stable on Polk Street near the
Fort Worth & Denver tracks. In just a few years he would be
one of the most influential men in Amarillo. The livery business grew and he added to it Amarillo's first streetcar service
operated with horses. He owned Amarillo's only coal yard
and became a stockholder of Amarillo's First National Bank
and later its president. It was known for more than fifty years
as the Fuqua Bank.[27]

Bones also returned to Amarillo in 1890 and went to work
for Fuqua on the ranch as his wrangler. Bones would be associated with Fuqua for many years, and he taught Fuqua's
son, Earl, how to ride a horse, as he did many of the children of prominent Amarilloans. By 1890 Amarillo had greatly changed from the first time Bones had been there. The
town had actually moved about a mile east of its original

location to what was the center of the Glidden and Sanborn Addition, thanks to the ingenuity of Henry B. Sanborn, who was determined to have a town on his property.

However, Bones was probably still not impressed with Amarillo for bronc busting and returned to his beloved Clarendon. He yearned for wide-open spaces. Then he worked his way back to the Pecos and broke horses for Bill Ross. Ross had worked for the large Hashknife operation about the same time as Bones, and likely they first became acquainted there. Bones often referred to Ross as an "old man," but he really wasn't much older than Bones. Ross arrived in the Pecos in 1886 and in 1890 he secured some backing and purchased a remnant of the old Hashknife Ranch, which had relocated its operation to Arizona. Ross established his headquarters at the old Dixie Land place.[28]

Meanwhile, Tommy Clayton had married and was involved in the town of Pecos where they purchased town

Bones Hooks as a cowboy in the Pecos region, circa 1890. *Courtesy of the Amarillo Public Library.*

lots. He and his wife participated in the organization of the first Sunday school in Pecos in 1890-91, which developed into the First Christian Church. Others had moved to town and among them was Clay Allison, the killer, a man who was deadly with a gun and used it when he was drinking heavily. But civilization was coming to the Pecos country and coming rapidly.

Bones remained single. There were few females in the region and fewer black females, if any at all. There was little hope of finding a wife in the area. As Bones noted, "When I was in all of these places, it'd be two or three years before I'd see another colored person." This didn't mean there weren't other blacks in the region, because a number of black cowboys worked in the Pecos country, as previously mentioned. But they weren't seen about much, and black frontier women were even less noticeable. In fact, there weren't a lot of women at all in the region in the pioneer days. Bones recalled Tommy Clayton's mother and wife, Ross's wife, an occasional female guest, and a few others. Clay Allison, the killer, was married with daughters and had moved to town, where Bones or any other black made only rare appearances, as they were not welcomed. The women on the ranches were white and married to the ranchers or the managers. The cowhands were all single men. Like other cowboys, Bones would have to go elsewhere if he wanted to find a wife.[29]

Since the cowboys did not have much opportunity to be around a proper lady, their ranch language was littered with all kinds of profanities. Some gave their horses names so vulgar that those names couldn't be called out in front of a female guest. Bones used to have fun with this when a woman arrived at the ranch. All of the cowboys would wash up, put on clean shirts, and be on their best behavior. Bones liked to get a cowboy in front of the visiting lady and ask, "Jim, what did you say your horse's name was?" Bones amusingly recalled that the cowboy's face would turn beet red because he was too ashamed to say his horse's name in front of the female company.[30]

Bones, Ross, and the Bull

No matter where Bones was employed, he always carried on the cowboy tradition of playing jokes and tricks. Sometimes such fun almost led to serious injury, yet the cowboys considered these situations hilarious and worth repeating over and over at the reunions. One such incident occurred when Bones was working for Bill Ross.

The outfit was working a wagon on the Black River and the boys were short of horses. Ross and Bones delivered some more horses, and as they returned to the headquarters, they stopped to drink some water at Screw Bean Springs. There was an old dugout nearby (which became an outlaw camp in the late 1890s) and Ross decided to go into the cool dugout and take a nap. He told Bones not to wake him "for nothing."

Meanwhile, Bones washed his feet and socks in the spring. Some wild cattle approached, but seeing Bones, they wouldn't come up and drink. There was a maverick bull (not branded) in the bunch, about fifteen or sixteen months old with unmarked ears. Bones hurriedly put on his socks and boots, ran to the dugout, and shouted, "Wake up!" He wisely stayed away from the entrance, as he knew the boss might throw something at him.

Ross demanded to know why he was disturbed when he had distinctly given an order not to wake him. Bones told Ross just to look down the creek, and Ross saw the big maverick bull. He got excited and told Bones to get his horse, because he wanted that bull as a gift for his son. Bones thought there wasn't anything prettier than an old cowman

and a big maverick. However, it was out of the branding season and somehow this one was missed by the ranchers. It was
too big a prize to let get away and Ross was going to brand
him, anyway. If he didn't, someone else was certain to. What
followed was amusing, but it could have turned out much
worse.

Bones brought up the horses and Ross told him to hold
on to the reins while he branded the bull. The cattle went
over the little rise with Ross on their heels and disappeared.
Bones patiently waited, and a short time later he heard Ross
yelling for help. When Bones rode over the hill, he saw that
the bull had gone through the loop, which had caught him
by one hind foot, and Ross had grabbed him by the tail in
order to "tail him down." But the bull kicked the rope off
and the tail was the only thing Ross had hold of as the bull
kicked, bawled, and tried to gore him. Bones recalled, "I
never saw a man hold of anything and crying for help that I
wouldn't get off and get a hold, too, unless it was a snake. So,
I jumped down and helped him."

Bones went to the side of the bull and grabbed him by
the horns to bulldog him. The first time the bull jumped, it
wasn't so high, but the second time was so high that Bones
wondered what had happened to the 190 pounds that was
supposed to be on the end of the tail. As Bones looked
back, to his surprise, Ross had let go of the tail and was running for the brush about seventy yards off. Bones thought,
"I'm colored. If this white man don't want this bull, I sure
don't."

Bones let go of the bull and took off after Ross as the bull
chased both of them. Bones was faster than Ross and overtook him. He reached the brush first, and as he stopped to
catch his breath, he heard a thump behind him. He whirled
around to see that the bull had hit his boss on the backside
and knocked him to the ground. The bull snorted, pawed,
and slobbered all over him. While the bull was occupied,

Bones slipped away and got the horses. He trotted back to where the bull still had Ross pinned down. Bones was in no hurry. It seemed as if he was enjoying himself. He finally asked, "Do you want me to rope him?"

"You fool!" Ross shouted. "What do you think I want you to do?"

Bones shrugged his shoulders. "A little while ago I thought you wanted me to throw him down and brand him, but as soon as I got hold of him you let loose. Now, if you don't want this bull, I sure don't want him." Then Bones roped the bull and pulled him away from Ross.

Ross stood up, his face covered with the bull's saliva, and they stared at each other for a moment, neither one saying a word. Then Bones burst out laughing. Ross wasn't amused and demanded to know what was so funny. Bones told him how funny he had looked with that bull standing over him. Ross gave Bones a dollar and told him not to tell anyone. He sure didn't want this embarrassing episode to get back to his rancher friends. Bones took the dollar and he didn't tell a soul, that is, until he saw someone. He explained, "It was just too good to keep."[31]

It was obviously a memory that Bones relished for years. Much later, at the cowboy and pioneer reunions, the story inevitably came up. If Bones didn't bring it up, one of the old cowmen never failed to ask about the time Ross and Bones tried to brand that maverick bull. Ross, of course, still admonished Bones for telling that story after he had paid him a dollar not to.

Bones was in Clarendon again in 1892 and was breaking horses for the JA, but Goodnight was no longer associated with the JA. He had dissolved his partnership with John Adair's widow, Cornelia Adair. Goodnight had been an efficient and trustworthy manager for John Adair and then Cornelia, and he was going to be difficult to replace. However, he did continue to manage Mrs. Adair's holdings until a suitable manager was found. In the dissolution, Mrs. Adair retained the Palo Duro lands that Goodnight first settled in 1876 and Goodnight received the Quitaque Ranch, also known as the Lazy F. The Goodnights then relocated to some land that they had purchased on the Fort Worth & Denver route where the town of Goodnight would grow up. Eventually, Goodnight sold the Quitaque in order to pay off some debts and bad investments, particularly the silver mines in Mexico. It was not the first time he had been hit hard. He had lost much in the early 1870s in Colorado, which forced him to find an investor, and that's when he made a deal with Adair. In 1890 he made another comeback as he and J. W. Thatcher organized the Goodnight-Thatcher Cattle Company. They survived the Panic of 1893, but in 1902 that partnership was also dissolved.[32]

Tommy Clayton

During the Panic of 1893, several English banks that had heavily invested in Panhandle ranches and banks crashed, rocking the Panhandle cattle industry. Amarillo struggled as a city and lost its incorporation, and its government offices were returned to the county's authority. However, Bones was in the Pecos at this time and his friend, Tommy Clayton, had a serious riding accident. Bones had been working the Davis Mountain Range when the news reached him via one of Clayton's hands or friends. Another cowboy, a hand named White, was already chosen to deliver the news to Clayton's wife. Bones picked some of the wild Davis Mountain white flowers that he and Tommy had always admired and sent them ahead with some of the boys. Bones recalled, "I didn't know how he was, if he was hurt bad; when the boys got there with the flowers Tommy was dead and Mrs. Clayton took the flowers. When they carried him to the cemetery his mother put one on the casket and on the grave." Later, Mrs. Clayton told Bones that he and Tommy weren't "one black and one white, nor two black and two white, but two friends." Bones was glad to accept it that way, "and ever since I've accepted it that way."[33]

Bones would never be as close to a white man as he had been with Tommy, and he wanted to show his respects at the funeral in Pecos. He went at his own peril, as many of the townsfolk were appalled at the presence of a black man at the white funeral.

Not long after the funeral, Bones returned to the Panhandle as he always did and spent more and more time in and near Clarendon, which he was now calling home. Clarendon was ever changing, but it remained a "Saints Roost" for the most part. They had a jail, but few were ever in it. There were saloons, but according to Bones, Clarendon's saloons were run by honest, decent men. He said:

> Clarendon saloon men would do to teach Sunday School. Jim Kane wouldn't let a boy buy liquor in his saloon. Cowboys came in, put a sack of money behind the counter and went off and left it there and never lost a cent.

Before the Methodists built a satisfactory church house, Mrs. Harwood Beville started a Sunday school in one of the saloons. On one occasion, a young Methodist preacher told an arriving settler of culture that her piano ought to be in the saloon, where it could be enjoyed on Sunday mornings.[34]

While Clarendon enjoyed a clean reputation, rustling continued to be a problem for all of the ranches. Sheriff Al Gentry of Clarendon did not seem to have many local criminals to put in jail, and cattle rustlers were not easy to catch over so much territory. So the cattlemen didn't wait for the sheriff to solve their problem. They took care of it themselves through vigilantes. In spite of his previous run-in with vigilantes, Bones became a respectable member of the organization. They were highly secretive and identified each other with a password. By using this password, news was sent out on when and where to meet. Then they converged on the suspected rustler and tried and hanged him. Bones often held the horses while the hanging occurred, and he took his place among the vigilantes with great pride.[35]

Not every trial ended with a man's neck in a noose, however. Bones remembered a case where they had caught up with a young rustler and sentenced him to hang. The young man wisely asked for two last requests. The first was to take off his boots, because he had promised his mother he wouldn't die with his boots on, meaning an untimely or dishonorable death. The second was that the rope be pulled by a man who had never stolen a cow or horse. The rope was never pulled, as there was not one vigilante among them who had not branded a maverick or stray out of season or with a brand already on it. He was then let go on his promise that he would never return to that part of the country.[36]

But don't be fooled. The vigilantes didn't let many go. Bones knew of at least fifteen thieves who were hanged by his group. He indicated that before he died, he would divulge the vigilantes' password for historical purposes and leave it at the Panhandle-Plains Historical Museum in Canyon, Texas. Unfortunately, there is no evidence that he ever did so. Perhaps in his old age he just forgot or the illness that ended his life came upon him too swift and hard.

The Last Trail Drive

Bones returned to the Pecos country again, breaking wild horses for Billie Johnson of the W Ranch. In 1895-96, he made his last cattle drive for the ranch. It was not destined for a market but instead the Diamond Tail Ranch, owned by Bill Curtis and headquartered in Collingsworth County, in the southeastern part of the Panhandle just north of Memphis, which was in Hall County. This herd was sizable—seventeen to eighteen hundred head of cattle—and it was probably one of the last big trail drives of this kind for this distance.[37]

Bill Curtis had connections with Charles Goodnight, William Ikard, Bose Ikard, and Oliver Loving, proving how small the vast Panhandle lands sometimes were. The Diamond Tail had purchased cattle from the JA Ranch in order to improve its stock, as Goodnight had been one of the leaders and innovators in stock breeding. Bones may have helped trail some cattle to the Diamond Tail in his previous employment on the JA, and if so, he would have realized that Bill Curtis, similar to Goodnight, John Chisum, and John Slaughter, hired a number of black cowboys. At the time of the drive, at least four blacks were employed on the Diamond Tail Ranch. The wranglers were Joe Barnes and George Shelton; the cooks were Bart Cleary and E. Brooks. Cleary was to remain loyally with the Diamond Tail until Curtis's death.

Following the trail drive to the Diamond Tail, Bones returned to Clarendon and stayed in the Panhandle for good this time. He never journeyed to the Pecos region again. He went to work for the RO Ranch as a bronc rider and became acquainted with bronc busters Frank White, Sr., and Joe Williams, the latter becoming a longtime friend. The RO was an interesting ranch, to say the least, owned by the eccentric Englishman Alfred Rowe. Rowe bought his first 8,000 acres in 1879 from Rev. Lewis H. Carhart and built his headquarters on the Big Skillet Creek in 1882. Other holdings of 64,000, 80,000, and 65,000 acres had already been acquired by the time Bones went to work for the RO.[38]

Bernard and Vincent, Alfred's brothers, came early into the partnership, but unlike with other foreign owners, this was not a corporation. It was a family enterprise, with the brothers borrowing money from relations back in England

in order to finance their dream. Bernard and Vincent, however, were less identified with the ranch than Alfred, who
put more time and effort into its operation. But with
Alfred's eccentricities, he disappeared for months at a time
without any explanation. It seems that he had severe bouts
of depression, but even then he was no fool, as he always left
the ranch in the hands of capable managers.

Alfred also differed from most foreign owners in that he
was not an absentee owner, and he actually knew something
about the cattle business. Nor was he pompous—he did not
refer to the cowhands as "cow servants," as did some foreign
owners, a title the cowboys detested. Upon arriving in the
Panhandle in 1878, he spent his first year working as a lowly
cowhand and learned about cattle before he ventured into
business for himself. He was as dedicated to the ranch as his
brothers were not, and he bought them out in 1898, becoming its sole owner.

Bones was fond of Alfred Rowe and always called him "Sir
Alfred," though no one else dared to. Alfred liked Bones,
too, and once confided in him that he wasn't respected in
England as he was in Texas. Bones made an effort to comfort Rowe's obvious depression. He replied, "Well, Sir
Alfred, why don't you just stay over here? You're a big man
over here." Then Alfred said, "I'm English. I suppose that's
the reason."[39]

Alfred Rowe was thirty-three when he married Constance
Ethel Kingsly. He brought her to the ranch, where their first
child was born . . . and died. Thereafter, Alfred sent her
home to England to give birth again, and he permanently
joined her in 1910. Yet he made yearly visits to the ranch,
and on one of these journeys he booked passage on the fate-
ful *Titanic* and perished at sea. He reportedly refused to take
his place on a lifeboat, as he was an excellent swimmer, and
allowed another his space.

The RO was a good place for Bones to be, as he got along

with Alfred Rowe quite well. Bones had several good memories there, but keeping in character, he preferred to tell the amusing ones. One involved a cattle buyer from Amarillo named Felix Franklin. Rowe sent Bones to pick Franklin up at the Clarendon train depot. Bones always "drove a spirited team," and as they left Clarendon, he decided to have a little fun. He let the horses run hard all the way to the ranch. As the story goes, the ride frightened Franklin so much that he tried to jump out of the buggy, but each time he rose, the horses "lunged forward and down plumped Mr. Franklin into his seat again," all the way to the ranch.[40]

Bones loved a good joke and having fun as much as anyone else, but he sometimes told tales that were not amusing. And when he did, it usually pointed out the difference between right and wrong. Perhaps the situation described below occurred on the RO, but it is difficult to determine, as Bones did not always identify the dates of his experiences.

Bones had not paid much attention to reading and writing when he was a youngster, but he was not completely illiterate. He could write his name and knew numbers and certain words, but his reading and writing skills were somewhat lacking. This was underscored one day when he received a letter on the ranch.

Many of the cowboys were illiterate, but others had a little education and a few even had a college background. Upon receiving this letter Bones asked a certain white cowboy to read it for him, but the cowboy flatly refused without the slightest explanation. Bones was taken aback and thought the cowboy was prejudiced. Bones knew how to deal with prejudiced cowboys. Thereafter, Bones mistreated him every chance he had, not by bodily injury or even malicious words, but by his rank. As wrangler, Bones was in charge of all of the horses. Each morning he brought the cowboys their working horses and each evening returned them to the corral and fed and took care of them. But this cowboy's best horses were purposely lost. Bones went out to the pasture and . . . just couldn't find them, it seemed.

This revealed Bones' disposition when he thought he was dealing with a bigot, but he was soon proven wrong about this particular cowhand. A day arrived when that white cowboy received a letter of his own and he had to ask someone to read it for him because he couldn't read. Bones then found out the real reason why the cowboy wouldn't—couldn't—read his letter. Bones took that incident to heart. He later said, "I found out not to judge anyone too quick before I found out all about him."[41]

In the twilight of his bronc-riding career, Bones worked for one of Clarendon's leading citizens, J. D. Jefferies, the same who later advised Bones to ride the outlaw horse in Pampa in 1910. Jefferies didn't start ranching near Clarendon until 1894. Before that he had been a surveyor for the Texas & Pacific Railroad. He later joined cattle drives to Fort Worth and Kansas. He followed that up as manager of the Turkey Track Division of the Matador Ranch in King and Motley counties. When he relocated to Clarendon, he not only was a successful cattleman, but he was civic minded and helped establish the first school of higher education in the Panhandle, which became Clarendon College.[42]

In the 1890s, Clarendon was not only the religious and educational center of the Panhandle but the center of the region's black population. The surrounding ranches had employed a number of black cowhands, cooks, and wranglers for years. After 1895, there were far more blacks in Donley County who were not cowboys, many of them women and children. The 1890 census reported about forty blacks in the Clarendon area; in 1900 there were approximately fifty.

Bones had become the leading black citizen in the county and was respected more than anyone else of his race because he was counted among the pioneers. In 1897, two white women, J. D. Stockman and Mrs. Hartman, were conducting a Sunday school for black children in the home of a Clarendon black citizen, Jane Briscoe. There were just a few Christians at this time other than Briscoe; they were Ed Thomas, Truman Thomas, Sally Ann Henderson, Mary King, and Ham Campbell. Being aware of the little Sunday school, Bones thought that his people ought to have their own church, with a minister of their own race, so he took it upon himself to find a preacher who might come to Clarendon. He found Rev. Sid Stevens of Fort Worth, and at the request of Bones they had their first preacher. Pastor Stevens remained in Clarendon and the St. Stephens Baptist Church was established, the first black church in the Panhandle.[43]

This was Bones' first civic and social accomplishment, but it would be far from his last. As the new century dawned, a new and amazing career was just on the horizon.

CHAPTER 3

Bones Hooks and Race Relations in the Pioneer Days

If a man was man enough to work on a ranch in the early days, he was too much of a man to abuse me.
—Bones Hooks

It has been commonly understood that as long as blacks and whites were working some of the same ranges and roundups, sleeping in the same bunkhouses and camps, and eating from the same mess tents and chuck wagons, there were going to be some racial problems. Part of the trouble was that many of the whites were former slave owners or the sons thereof, and most of the black ranch hands were former slaves or the sons thereof. Therefore, prejudice was a reality, and there is no doubt that a number of Southern whites harbored a deep-seated hostility due to the Civil War and Reconstruction, not only towards blacks but Northern whites as well. They squarely placed blame on blacks and Northerners for the condition of the postwar South, and that attitude carried over for many generations.

In view of this, the life and times of Mathew ("Bones") Hooks read somewhat differently from those of other black cowboys. Bones Hooks' experiences as a bronc rider and civic leader are unique in that he found ways to overcome prejudice and help his people with only his wit, honesty, and ability to make lasting friends.

Information about Bones' experiences with race relations comes mostly from his own words. Despite prejudice on the range, which he readily admitted that he hated, he lived in a similar manner as most of the cowboys, except he never took up liquor and tobacco. Most remarkable, however, is his statement that he faced little prejudice in the pioneer days. Bones maintained that it took a certain breed of man to work on a ranch and get along with others in those days, and an unspoken code of sorts ruled the frontier. In essence, a ranch hand had to be tough, durable, and basically uncomplaining. It wasn't a life for the timid, and there was no long-term financial reward. The work was often seasonal and many of the cowboys were transient with no place to lay their heads. Just a small percentage remained year round on the ranch and the rest moved on or took odd jobs in town for the winter. Another number traveled from range to range looking for work, and if none was found, at least they were allowed to partake of the chuck wagon. It was unthinkable in the pioneer days not to feed a cowboy, regardless of his color. Even the settlers would do that. A black cowboy might not get a bed in the house, but he was certain to be fed.

Bones referred to the pioneer days as the time before the railroads were built through the region, bringing in settlers and establishing towns that changed the landscape and character of the wide-open range. Although much has been uncovered about black history in these times, not much has been said about racism in the pioneer days other than the educated guesses of scholars. Relatively few documents exist demonstrating that blacks spoke out on prejudice. Most experiences of black cowboys have been told through the eyes of white contemporaries.

Just recently has the story of black cowboys been told,

though briefly, in new books such as *Black Cowboys of Texas*. However, more often than not, the writer speaks for the cowboy and not always accurately. Some of the older books, such as *A Vaquero in the Brush Country*, included black cowboys in descriptions of the everyday work, fun, and fundamentals of the ranch life but still referred to them as *niggers*. An example of the white perspective is that of Cecil Bonney, a contemporary of Ad Jones, who stated that the word "nigger" was used during pioneer days with respect and affection. Bonney may have intended it that way, but that does not mean that Jones or any other black cowboy took it that way. Scholars point out that no matter how it was meant, it was an affront to all black cowboys. But blacks were usually silent on the issue, probably because their opinions were rarely sought. Even Bones Hooks, who was often called Nigger Bones in those days, did not reflect upon the issue in his interviews, but he had much to say about other things. As often as Bones was interviewed in his lifetime, his silence about the term seems strange, unless he considered it too trivial to bring up.

It should be noted that there were some unique relationships between black ranch hands and the ranch owners. Some of these relationships lasted twenty, thirty, and even forty years. Charles Goodnight considered Bose Ikard the most trusted man he ever knew; Bart Cleary was devoted to Bill Curtis of the Diamond Tail Ranch; 7D George Adams was a loyal hand for C. F. Cox; Ad Jones was with George Littlefield of the LFD most of his ranch life; and Bones Hooks was closer to Tommy Clayton than he was to any other white man, although his association with Clayton was far shorter than any of the other relationships just mentioned.[1]

Bones had little in common with most of the other black cowboys. He was not born a slave and he had been exclusively around white ranchers since he was about ten years old. He worked for numerous ranchers wherever breaking horses took him. He was never a loyal employee in the sense of Ad Jones or Bose Ikard, both of whom had been born into slavery, and Bones was a transient cowboy most of his ranch life.

It appears that four things helped Bones be as free spirited as he was and behave as if he was not a different race than the whites. First, he had no slave history and did not stay around Robertson County long, which was a racially volatile place. The West Texas and Panhandle regions, where he predominantly lived since the age of fifteen, had no slave history. Blacks were also fewer in numbers there and posed less of a threat than areas with large black populations. Finally, everything was new in the region, especially the Panhandle. The pioneers made it as they wanted it to be, and as one historian pointed out, "it was neither northern nor southern nor foreign."[2]

Yet cruel prejudice existed, because people brought it from where it had been taught to them. Bones faced it shortly after arriving in the Pecos with J. R. Norris and the JRE outfit. It had a lot to do with him becoming such a great bronc rider. Bones said, "The cowboys would put me on the horses and they would throw me off hardly before I got in the saddle, but the boys kept putting me on them and they kept throwing me off until finally they could find none that I could not ride."[4]

This was not unlike the harsh treatment Birl Brown received in Clarendon. After Birl had been taken to Clarendon by his kidnappers, he ended up on the Half Circle K Ranch owned by Bill Koogle, a former freighter. Red Williams was the foreman of the ranch and a real tough man. The top bronc buster was a young daredevil named Dave Buchanan. Williams wanted a high-spirited horse and he ordered Buchanan to break it. Buchanan refused because it was the custom for everyone to break his own personal horse. But still Red Williams wouldn't do it himself. He had the boys put young Birl in the saddle, and he tied the boy's feet under the horse's belly. Buchanan protested because he realized that the horse was likely to kill Birl. He said, "Handling him is a real man's job." It certainly wasn't a job for a youngster like Birl. The horse beat Birl so badly that he could not hold up his head, and blood oozed from his mouth and nose with each violent thud. Buchanan couldn't stand it any longer. He roped the horse, even with the chance of it falling on Birl and crushing him. It made one bad stumble and Birl fell free. Buchanan picked Birl up in his arms, carried him into the house, and said to Red Williams, "Any fellow who would pull a trick like that is the damnedest low down skunk alive."[4]

Bones' situation on the JRE could have been like this, but Bones needed no one to strap him on to a horse. Every time he was thrown, he was ready to get back on. He had real grit, as the cowboys were finding out. Young blacks and runaways were often used to test the most dangerous situations, like trying a swollen river or riding the meanest horses. Bones understood that making him a bronc rider was partly due to prejudice. He said, "They were trying to get me throwed, but they made a rider out of me. . . . They made me the best bronc rider in the country, but they weren't trying to make me a rider."[5]

The prejudiced cowboys learned to respect Bones, for he proved his courage time and time again riding the meanest horses in the region. In doing so, he also made lasting friends, and when people spoke of the kid named Bones, it was with high praise for a teenager who broke outlaw horses that most grown men could not.

When Bones visited his parents, he found a lot more prejudice in East Texas than he did in the Pecos country. Klan-like groups existed all over the area. There was prejudice in the Panhandle, too, in towns like Mobeetie and Memphis. Other towns like Tascosa were just too wild for him. He found Clarendon to his liking, as mentioned before, but he returned to the Pecos country: "I liked the Pecos so well that I went back to it."[6]

As Bones became a man, according to age and maturity, he didn't have much trouble with prejudiced cowhands and when he did, he knew how to deal with it. He acted like a cowboy—not a black or white cowboy, but just a cowboy— and he took his place among them quite seriously. This is where Bones' life does not read like most of the black cowboy experiences that have recently been published. Neither was he at odds with the whites, except on rare occasions, and he used friendships to overcome prejudice. He proved that friendships were more powerful than the fist or gun. This may have been due to his father's influence. Bones said:

> You can keep friends always. You may lose everything, but you can't lose that. There will be nothing in the world like old friends. . . . Friends can be more useful to you than anything.[7]

Bones and Arthie

While working for Bill Ross, Bones once made a bad judgment that proved that his position among the cowboys was rock solid, due to the friends that he had made. This happened when Arthie (Arthur), Bill Ross's younger brother, was cooking for the outfit. Bones rode back to the wagon one day to get something and found Arthie practicing roping. Bones jumped off his horse and showed him how it was done. Arthie just couldn't get the hang of it, and Bones told the boss's little brother that he'd never make a "real cowhand." Arthie was perturbed, to say the least, and he demanded to know why Bones had said that.

"Because," Bones answered.

That made Arthie just the more angry. He walked up to Bones "all fierce-like" and said, "How do you know I won't?"

Bones suddenly realized that he was in a tight position and needed some backing. "Because John says you won't," Bones said. John was John Fuller, the foreman. And that's when Arthie really blew up. He kicked over the pots and pans at the fire where he had been cooking supper, then grabbed his gun and said, "I'll shoot him on sight!"

Bones didn't doubt that Arthie meant every word, so he jumped on his horse and rode out to the others to warn them. Bones went to Bill Ross and explained what Arthie said he'd do. Ross wanted to know why Bones had told him such a thing. "Because John said it," he simply answered. But John Fuller denied it, and all of the cowboys denied hearing him say it. It seemed that Bones was standing out on a limb.

There was nothing for Bill Ross to do except go back to the camp and talk to Arthie. Bones warned him again that he would shoot. Ross, however, was certain that his brother wouldn't. He also ordered Bones to come along, since he instigated the whole mess with his loose tongue. Bones didn't want to go but didn't have any choice, since the boss told him to.

When they got there, Ross asked his brother why he kicked over supper. Arthie replied it was because John Fuller said he'd never make a "real cowhand." Ross told his brother that it just wasn't true, but Arthie insisted Fuller had said it, because "the nigger boy don't lie." Ross talked with his brother some more and told him that if he didn't want to cook he'd take him back to town. That sounded like a reasonable compromise to Arthie, but before they started back to town Ross ordered Bones to get supper ready. He cooked for the outfit until they could find a new cook.[8]

Bones learned another character lesson that day. He said, "It don't pay to repeat what folks say about somebody."[9]

The incident pointed out a few interesting things. "Nigger" was in common use by whites, and Bones was not singled out because of his color. He seems to have been a legitimate member of the outfit and not someone just tolerated. He was punished with cooking duties because he was partly responsible for the loss of the cook. The carrying of tales had obviously disrupted the outfit, and yet he told this story with humor, just as the white cowboys probably would have done. If there was racism in this incident, Bones never looked for it nor even considered it. Racism would find him often enough.

Another circumstance was quite the opposite. In this incident Bones knew he was facing prejudice outright. It occurred on what Bones described as a "cold bitter night." The wind was howling and frigid, making both work and sleep most difficult. Bones made a habit of carrying plenty of bedding just for times like these and he also carried a tent or tarp to protect against rain. However, a certain white cowboy in the outfit didn't have much of a bedroll—just one blanket, actually—and on this cold night it surely wasn't enough. The white cowhand kept pulling his blanket up around his neck and shivering while looking over at Bones. Bones was the only one who had enough blankets for two, but the cowboy was prejudiced and initially didn't want to ask Bones to share. Finally he couldn't stand it any longer and swallowed his pride a bit. He called to Bones, "Looks like we're going to have to put our beds together to keep warm." Bones replied, "I'm already warm." The prejudiced cowhand shivered a little while longer as Bones made no attempt to share. Finally, he had had enough and told Bones to move over. "Here I come," he announced. A fight or worse might have followed, but Bones allowed the prejudiced cowboy to crawl under the blankets with him, and they put the cold cowboy's one blanket on top of the rest. They made strange bedfellows, but of this night Bones said, "We slept warm and neither of us was hurt."[10]

Best Friends

Bones was a wise man. He realized that nature was far

more powerful than human prejudice and would defeat it better than any intellectual argument ever could. Devastating heat, droughts, blizzards, cold winds, rain, hail, tornadoes, grass fires, and so forth demanded that some of the race barriers be broken down, for these people needed each other in order to merely survive. Perhaps the prejudiced cowboy decided that Bones wasn't so bad after sharing the bedroll with him, and the cold would have been largely responsible for that.

If Bones went easily through the gate, so to speak, it may have been because he had lived with whites for so long. He said, "I see white and think white," which may have been why he moved so freely in the predominantly white ranching culture of the Pecos and the Panhandle regions. It was also the reason for his friendship with Tommy Clayton. But something happened that changed that relationship and Bones' perspective on seeing white and thinking white, forever.

It has already been established that Bones and Tommy Clayton were extremely close friends and went everywhere together until Clayton's untimely death. However, one time they were camping with a white boy from Georgia who was going home for Christmas to marry his sweetheart, and he wanted Clayton to go with him. He showed Clayton a picture of his girl. Clayton admired the picture, but not once did he show it to Bones nor even slightly turn his hand so Bones might see. Bones was not permitted to be a part of that bonding. He was on the outside looking in.

As close as Bones and Clayton were, Clayton may have felt similar to the Georgia boy, that showing the picture to a Negro would defile this Southern belle. Or maybe he was just intimidated by the boy from Georgia and his Southern ways. A third scenario could be that he just didn't consider revealing the picture to Bones. But Clayton probably realized that letting Bones see the girl's picture would be an insult to his friend from Georgia. Instead, it was Bones who was hurt and insulted. Bones recalled:

There was just something between us. I knowed I was colored. He couldn't take me to his friend's house to visit
and he couldn't show me his friend's sweetheart's picture.
Just then I knew I was colored and he was white.[11]

Bones and Tommy Clayton had been more than friends;
they were partners in the horse business up until this time.
The partnership probably ended soon after the incident.
Bones understood that friendship with a white boy could
only go so far. Friendship out on the range or the scarcely
settled frontier was one thing, but going to Georgia with
Clayton and the other white boy presented a list of other
realities that Bones did not want to confront.

Yet this did not turn Bones against Clayton or other whites.
It just opened his eyes. Clayton couldn't stand up for Bones
and their friendship because he was weak. He was unable to
withstand the cultural pressure, especially from many
Southerners. He was unable to choose friendship over bigotry.
Instead, he faltered and submitted to racism. Clayton lost an
opportunity to act honorably on friendship not inequality.

The situation may have been the reason for Bones' sudden
homesickness and his departure from the Pecos for awhile. By
the time he returned to the Pecos, the friendship had obviously cooled somewhat, but it did continue. Bones refrained from
making any harsh judgments on his friend. He spoke openly
of the incident but still observed, "As far as he [Clayton] was
personally concerned, he would always stand by me." This
points to Bones' uncompromising loyalty and his grasp of
Clayton's predicament. More importantly, Bones was willing to
reconcile, a gift that would greatly aid him in the future.[12]

A few years later when Clayton was killed in the riding
accident, Bones began the cowboy tradition of sending
white flowers to the families of pioneers and others who
were worthy of being honored. Tommy Clayton had been
the first so honored, but wherever Bones went he found a

number of white men he respected, and he made a point to honor the family when such good men passed on. At the same time, he was building a reputation beyond that of a bronc rider. He was becoming civic minded and generous.

Bones started calling Clarendon home shortly after 1886 but would return to the Pecos for several more years. Few blacks were in the Panhandle in these times and some whites said that he couldn't stay in this country, that "they wouldn't let a Negro stay." But Bones didn't believe it and never accepted it. Some fifty years after coming to the Panhandle, he said, "That is the reason I'm here . . . and I still don't believe it."[13]

Bones once remarked, "The thing that has made the Panhandle the White Spot [bright spot] of the nation is the spirit—the spirit of the pioneers—the spirit that believes things is going to be better tomorrow." Another time he said, "The Panhandle has the finest families of any place in the country. . . . Congenial relations have been built up because of the type of white men living here." Of course, he was referring to the families who came and settled the region with blood, sweat, and dust. He pioneered the region with them, and he knew what kind of people he was among.[14]

For example, someone once fired a gun through a window of a black man's house and killed his wife, which caused race problems at the time. Bones did not identify the place; he only said it was in "another locality." However, there was the problem of where to bury her, as blacks were not welcome in certain parts of the region. So Bones went to his friends in Clarendon and got permission to bury her there. This was probably the first public burial of a black person in this part of the country.[15]

Ranch Life

In view of everything that has been said about the Panhandle, it is clear that Bones chose to live in this region not because of the abundance of work but because of the kind of people living here. He couldn't get away from prejudice, but he seems to have believed that there were enough decent people in the Panhandle that racism could be overcome. He said many times, "In the pioneer days there was little race prejudice here. When a range rider rode up to a house he didn't look for color, but for a human being."[16]

It was a lonely place, for many neighbors were a good distance away. Only in the small towns was there a regular gathering of folks. Books and movies have long ingrained into our heads how dangerous was the wild, wild West. Despite this representation, there were decent men and women, and law and order were very much in evidence. Nesters and settlers had more to do with taming the West than the Colt and Winchester. When they came with wives and children, they easily outnumbered the lawless ones. However, it was the women settlers who demanded law and order, churches, and schools, and their husbands got those things for them. But what of the wild towns like Dodge City, Tascosa, and Tombstone, where there were cemeteries as testimonies of lawlessness? They surely existed and saw their share of evil deeds. But John Arnot, who was a cowboy, rancher, and civic leader, trailed cattle to Dodge City and frequented Tascosa, and he wrote that in over fifty years he had never seen a gunfight in any of the wild, wild towns where he had been.

Some of the cowboys were like Bones Hooks and did not smoke, drink, throw away money on loose women, nor use their guns to solve their troubles. Bones carried a gun mainly to shoot a threatening snake or wolf, and wherever he went he made friends—not enemies. His only real vice was gambling on horse races and he was a very good judge of horse flesh. Recall also that he had an upbringing that was deep with reverence for God. Although quite simple, his church was the wide-open spaces, the Bible that he carried in his saddlebag, and the blanket of stars that constantly reminded him that God was always near.

There were many reasons why Bones advocated the Panhandle as the best place of all, even with the prejudice that existed in certain towns like Mobeetie. But it is reasonable to say that the ranches in the Panhandle and also the Pecos region presented a far more equal environment than any other in the country. Even though equality was not a goal, ranch rules in the pioneer days were very evenhanded. The ranch managers saw that these were enforced, without regard to color, for the profitable and efficient operation of the outfit. For instance, ranch rules prohibited liquor and gambling on the property. The XIT had their ranch rules in writing. The cowboys read it, or had it read to them, and each one agreed to the rules by signing a copy. Charles Goodnight never rehired a man who defied his ranch rules and even fired his own brother-in-law for gambling.

While employed on most of these ranches, all the cowboys slept in the same bunkhouses and campgrounds. They ate in the same mess tents or off the same chuck wagons. As George McJunkin, a black cowboy, was surprised to learn, when mess was called, it was first come first serve. But when he was in an establishment in town, he usually had to wait until all of the white customers were served.

However, the hours were long, the work was hard, and the wages were low. A cowhand made about thirty-five dollars per month with room and board and the use of company horses, while a wagon boss earned about fifty dollars a month with the same privileges. A bronc buster made about twenty-five dollars a month, or as Bones indicated, he could make three dollars for every horse he broke. Blacks still got the short end of the stick, often assigned the hardest, dirtiest work and extra duties such as taking care of the rancher's children. Bones taught many ranchers' children to ride a horse, and in that sense, he was still rocking the cradle.

Blacks also did not have much hope of becoming range bosses or foremen, except on rare occasions. Jim Perry, the longtime XIT hand, said, "If it weren't for my damned old black face, I'd have been boss of one of these divisions long ago." Likewise, Ad Jones, recognized as one of the best cowboys in the Pecos region, was not a top hand because of his color. Yet he did command his own outfit of black cowboys from South Texas, and his outfit was inferior to none.[17]

Bones said there wasn't much racial prejudice in the pioneer days and he maintained that throughout his life. The unequal practices regarding foreman and manager positions were quite evident, but Bones never sought any of those positions and must have been referring to how he was personally treated. He didn't even seem to take the term "nigger" seriously at the time, but in later years he would consider it a degradation to his people.

Charles Warford, who personally knew Bones and admired him, could relate to some of his claims about prejudice taking a backseat during difficult times. Warford served in the navy during World War II and was on a ship that had some "rednecks" aboard from West Virginia. But something strange happened when the torpedoing started. There was no racist aboard. Everyone was united in fighting the common enemy, and any prejudice was set aside.[18] So it was between Bones and racist cowboys when they faced dangers like tornadoes or blizzards out on the range.

There have been many opinions and theories about life in the Old West, from scholars to readers of Western fiction, but they are usually based on the words of white cowboys. Bones Hooks' memories provide a fresh outlook, indeed. He boldly suggested that ranch life in the pioneer days was far fairer than recent writings indicate. New books cite severely racist incidents and hiring practices. Whites are still speaking for black cowboys, it seems, because blacks were silent on their place in history—not because they refused to speak, but because the white writers didn't ask their opinions and thoughts in the pioneer days.

However, Bones did speak, and he was right when he said, "History has not been recorded as it should have been." He also commented:

> The pioneers made lots of history, but recorded little of it. Later, historians had to draw on their imaginations and it is difficult to get the real facts. In the old days, no one asked a man his name or where he was from. He just accepted him as a man, a friend.[19]

That was the code under which Bones operated, and apparently so did many others in the pioneer days. He acknowledged prejudice but insisted a prejudiced cowboy couldn't stay on a ranch very long if he didn't change his ways, accept others, and pull his own weight. Respect was greatly prized in the days shortly after emancipation. The personal gains blacks made in the pioneer days were truly remarkable, considering there were no civil-rights workers and no one thought about equality and discrimination. They were simply trying to do the best job they could and living a life that many weren't tough enough to live. No wonder they were called "the rare breed."

Bones Hooks spoke at length about the importance of respect, honor, and friendship in those days. Much can be learned from his life and times. As noted earlier, Bones' life may not read like that of other black cowboys, but it doesn't make it any less true. Bones Hooks was certainly a rare individual who conquered almost every situation and barrier that presented itself, and he did it with his wit and genuine decency.

Bones Hooks undoubtedly personified the true "cowboy code." He stands today as a great example of everything honorable about the cowboy way of life.

PART II

CHAPTER 4

Personal and Cultural Transformation

I have tried to be Indian and I have tried to be white. I got
a strain of white blood in me, but my skin is colored. Now
I'm reconciled . . . to be colored. . . . I ain't ashamed of
my color anymore.

—Bones Hooks

As the nineteenth century came to a close, Bones was living quietly in Clarendon. He was thirty-three years old and
unmarried. There were few black women in the Panhandle
whom he might marry, but he had no intention of making
his home elsewhere. He didn't care that the region was predominantly white and wasn't going to change for many
decades. He loved Clarendon and the people of the Plains.
He often pointed out to others that the Panhandle had the
"finest families of any place in the country."[1]

Bones referred to Clarendon as the "white spot of civilization" because of the ratio of whites to other races there. And
when he spoke so glowingly of the Panhandle, he was actually speaking of the people in and around his adopted
hometown, Clarendon.[2]

In 1900 Bones' life was to take a drastic turn. He went to
Ennis, Texas, where he courted Indiana ("Anna") Crenshaw,

who became his bride at the age of nineteen. He probably needed a little civilization in his own life, and the bronc rider who tamed wild horses had the wildness in him tamed just a bit. Shortly after they were married, Bones retired from bronc busting, as that occupation was hard on a couple. They went to work at a new hotel in Amarillo called the Elmhurst, "taking care of the linens."[3]

This was very different for Bones. But he understood that when a black cowboy quit being a cowboy, there weren't a lot of other opportunities for him, and he certainly wasn't going to be revered as he was in his former occupation. The only jobs available to blacks outside of ranch work were hotel work, the railroads, and domestic service. None of these appealed to him, and it seems he was not quite ready to give up bronc busting and wanted to try it professionally. A big rodeo was held in Denver that year and he wanted to compete. The rodeo was quickly becoming a great Western event that showcased the cowboys' skills. The first rodeo might have been held in Canadian, Texas, or in Pecos. Another rodeo was held in Mobeetie in 1884, where an unnamed black cowboy won the title. Denver held a big rodeo in 1896 that had been well received and that permitted cowboys of all races to compete. Blacks did well there against their white and Mexican counterparts. Therefore, Bones had high expectations for the wild-bronc-riding event. However, he was rudely awakened when he arrived to find that the rules had been changed, affecting the complexion of the rodeo for years to come. Blacks were not allowed to compete in 1900. It became a white affair, unjustly turning its back on black cowboys who had helped settle and shape the West.

This eliminated some of the greatest cowboys from competition and of course guaranteed that whites dominated the circuit. But those who were competing knew that some of the best were only watching and that any championship was only half of a championship without the black cowboys. Samuel Thomas Privet, otherwise known as Booger Red, who was considered by many the world's best bronc rider for a quarter of a century and whose fame was legendary in Texas, knew what an injustice had been done to the black cowboy. He was once asked what he thought about Bones Hooks, and he answered, "What I can ride in the saddle, Bones can ride bareback." Booger Red was not going to change things, but he did acknowledge Bones and gave him the respect due him. And that's all Bones ever got from the rodeo circuit.[4]

When Bones returned to Amarillo, he changed bed sheets for a few years but was never far from horses, as he taught many of the white children to ride and was at every horse race he could find. However, he continued to yearn for ranch work and began looking for a spread to purchase, following his many years of saving and thrifty living. The great land boom in the Panhandle was opening up vast lands to settlers and breaking up many of the large ranches, in particular the foreign-owned operations.

Some thought they'd never see the day when nesters would close in on cattlemen, but a lot of things happened to bring this about. The railroads built lines across the Panhandle, and towns developed on the right-of-way route, like Amarillo. In addition, the state of Texas stepped in to ensure that settlers weren't driven out by cattle barons like Charles Goodnight, and the cattlemen's stranglehold on the grazing lands were broken in part by the Homestead Laws. These laws gave railroads tracts of land along the their routes, which they sold to settlers or as town sites. This helped finance railroad construction, since the land grants had long ago been used up and discontinued. The Public Land Policy Act and its revision (1885-87) also gave an individual who lived on the land for three years the opportunity to buy a minimum of 160 acres, or one section (640 acres), of agricultural land at two cents per acre with dry land and three cents per acre with water. These policies, in conjunction with the land companies, boosters, and merchants who set up new businesses along the railroad routes, helped populate the Panhandle, which in turn aided with financing the construction of the railroad line.[5]

The ranchers had enjoyed a grip on the public land, leasing it with the influence of state politicians they helped get elected. But when the new land laws went into effect, there was nothing the powerful ranchers could do. These laws prohibited foreign corporate buyouts and restricted leasing agreements to "five years at four cents an acre with the understanding that agricultural land could be sold to settlers at any time." Another aid to settlers was the 1895 Four Section Act and its 1897 revision, which disrupted the ranchers' endless leasing of public lands through relatives and employees.[6]

Certain acts of nature also helped break up ranches into small farms. Summer droughts and harsh winters, especially the winter of 1886-87, brought ranchers financial woe, and dropping cattle prices and the Economic Depression of 1893 hit the ranches and railroads hard. About this time, the big sale of Panhandle and South Plains lands began, lasting approximately until the end of World War I. By this time, the landscape of the Panhandle had drastically changed as well, as wheat competed with cattle as the top money source.

It would seem that with this growth in the Panhandle, the area would open up to black farmers, ranchers, and settlers. Yet it never happened. The businesspeople and the types of settlers who were pouring into the region were not the kind that Bones referred to as pioneers. In fact, real-estate companies led a movement to create a white utopia of sorts, and they were open about it. They often advertised as far away as New York and London with circulars that read like this one from the Dilliard-Powell Land Company: *Come and get a home among a good class of people who are liberal, hospitable, charitable, law abiding and where peace and harmony abounds and where there are no negroes.* The Short and Williams Land Company wrote: *Our population is entirely white and we are glad that is the case.*[7] The real-estate companies did not consider blacks, Chinese, Japanese, Mexicans, and Native Americans "real Americans" and consequently did not desire them as land buyers. Some whites were also rejected as potential landowners for financial reasons, since it was recommended that a serious purchaser have no less than $500 in cash and as much as $5,000![8]

Bones felt the brunt of the discrimination. He was a pioneer and had rubbed shoulders with the likes of Charles Goodnight, Alfred Rowe, W. H. Fuqua, Lee Bivins, and many more who had risked all to settle this land. He actually had more right to the land than the newcomers. He helped bring civilization to the Panhandle and was one of its strongest advocates, but he was denied any right to purchase land. He had the right color of money but not the right color of skin. Instead, he ended up purchasing a ranch near Roswell, New Mexico, about 1907. The ranch had little water and needed much improvement before it could successfully operate.[9]

Bones Becomes a Railroad Porter

Bones soon realized that he needed more income to make the New Mexico ranch work. As he returned to Amarillo, he followed in other black cowboys' footsteps by taking a job as a porter on the Santa Fe Railroad. But he would soon have double pay as he also handled the more dangerous job of Pullman. A Pullman worked the Pullman cars, managing all of those passengers' requests, and was on duty almost constantly. There was a lot of competition among Pullmen, as well as fights. Bones often joked that he went to work for the railroad because Henry Ford put him out of the bronc-busting business, but he admitted that he took the job because he needed more money to invest into his ranch. Unfortunately, his dream of being a horse rancher never came true, as he took a greater interest in other things in his life.[10]

Bones would hold the railroad job for about nineteen years, and he saw settlers, many foreign, arriving daily in the Panhandle to purchase farms. He was an eyewitness to the landscape's gradual change from endless acres of grazing lands to wheat and cotton fields. In Amarillo alone, at least four railcars of prospective buyers arrived each month. Bones realized that not only was the ranch way of life vanishing but so were some of the great pioneer ranches. Even the three-million-acre XIT Ranch was broken up by 1912, although it would be many years before it was all sold off.

In 1910, Bones' life was altered in a dramatic way. He rode that outlaw horse in Pampa on that late-winter day in March. He became a sort of celebrity. People recognized him on the street and wanted to shake his hand. They wanted to hear about the pioneer days, which he was always willing to recall. He frequently saw old friends on the trains he was working, and they never failed to reminisce about the days gone by. He never missed the cowboy and pioneer reunions and was always popular at those events, which emulated the pioneer days with horseracing, barbecues, campfires, and the telling of old stories that seemed to grow taller each year. He renewed his friendships with the Bivinses, Fuquas, and others of the Panhandle and those like Bill Ross of the Pecos. Bones was held in high esteem by the pioneers because he was one of them. The newcomers didn't know what it was like when the Panhandle had few towns and few people and what kind of man or woman it took to live out here in this vast prairie land back then.

Through it all, Bones wanted to express his affection and respect for his fellow pioneers. He remembered the white flowers he presented to Tommy Clayton's mother, in the deep-rooted cowboy tradition of giving honor to whom honor was due. So when a pioneer died, Bones presented a white flower to the family. He explained what was behind his action: "I like to give them [the flowers] to distinguished people because of the meaning the flower has for me and because of my respect for the white people [the pioneers]."[11]

In Amarillo and Clarendon, Bones' status was clear. All public places were accessible to him due to his fame and pioneer friends. He was placed on a pedestal by whites who greatly admired him. It is safe to say that during these times most of his friends were white. Few black pioneers in the Panhandle remained as he had.

However, while working for the railroad, Bones got to know some of his own people, men such as Phillip Shorten, Martin Jefferson, and Brother Jerry Calloway. Through these men, Bones would reconnect with his past and see the plight of blacks without facing racism himself.

When Bones went to work for the Santa Fe Railroad in 1909, there was no black neighborhood in Amarillo. Most lived in servant quarters in the affluent part of town where they worked. Others worked in the downtown hotels, primarily the Amarillo Hotel, which was owned by H. P. Canode, who provided housing for his employees in an older hotel called the Annex. Some worked for the railroads as did Bones, and the railroads had their own housing near the tracks. The servant quarters were terribly overcrowded by 1913 and housing became available to them on the first and second blocks of Harrison and Van Buren streets along the Fort Worth & Denver tracks. The houses were old and had been mostly occupied by Europeans and the elderly. Blacks began moving into the vacant houses in this section, and their leaders moved swiftly to organize an elementary school, simply called the "Colored Public School." A year later the Fred Douglass School was established, and

Early Christians of Amarillo, 1914. *Courtesy of the Panhandle-Plains Historical Museum, Canyon, Tex.*

although the Amarillo School District minutes do not name any of the black leaders, it is a consensus among the oldest black residents alive that Bones Hooks was one of them. It seems logical that, with Bones' influence among whites, his race might turn to him for leadership.

A year later Bones was part of a group that appears to have been one of the first black Christian assemblies in Amarillo. In all probability they were some of the original members of the Mt. Zion Missionary Baptist Church. A photograph clearly shows Bones' early involvement in the affairs of the black community,[12] but even at this time he was not living among his own people in the growing little neighborhood along the Fort Worth & Denver tracks called "the Flats."

Widower

Bones and his wife, Anna, lived for some time on South

Fillmore in the affluent section in a rear house (servant quarters) behind Dr. John Bedford, surgeon-in-charge at the Elmhirst Hospital. Anna was probably a domestic for Dr. Bedford but did not live in his house, and Bones did not allow her to sleep over in any of the white folks' homes where she might have worked. Not long after moving from the Fillmore residence, they were found to be living in East Amarillo on Johnson Street, a considerable distance from Amarillo's affluent section and the Flats. This was near the Santa Fe Depot and may have been railroad housing.

In 1920, Bones' life drastically changed again. Anna suddenly died on January 20 at the age of thirty-nine. Naturally, Bones was devastated. He had deeply loved her and she had been a good wife to him. Yet they had been complete opposites. She didn't like jokes when they first got married, and joking was a big part of Bones' life. But Bones said that after awhile "she got where she could beat me telling them." He also remarked, "She was a good woman, a good cook, and a good housekeeper." These were extremely important things in that era. He trusted her implicitly and depended on her intuition. He declared, "When she said not to do a thing, I'd better listen. She seemed to know ahead." He missed her terribly and would never find anyone else with whom he could get along so well. Bones was fifty-two when Anna died. She was buried in the segregated section of the Llano Cemetery, where Bones had his own plot prepared right beside hers.[13]

Around the time of Anna's premature death, Amarillo experienced significant population growth. Potter County had 16 or 17 blacks in 1900; this number jumped to about 149 in 1910 and over 300 by 1920.[14] The servant quarters in the wealthy white section continued to be overcrowded, and the Flats neighborhood was rapidly getting that way. Many whites viewed the black population growth as a threat to their own control and domination. Prejudice increased, and as one old-timer put it, "blacks were sport." The women were especially harassed downtown on Polk Street as they went to and from the hotels and businesses where they were employed. Brother Jerry Calloway was a big and powerful man and used to protect them with a whip, with which he was reported to be an expert. Some said he was so good he could thread a needle with it. Oscar D. Shorten said that, as far as he was concerned, "Brother Jerry was the bravest man in Amarillo, Texas."[15]

Bones was far from idle after Anna's death. His loneliness lasted approximately two years, until he met a woman in the Flats named Minnie Bishop, who had a young daughter named Georgia. He married Minnie in 1922, but it was a rocky marriage from start to finish that was destined to fail. They were not suited for one another and Bones had a calling that was far different from what Minnie had expected. One of her biggest complaints was that Bones was always gone to this reunion or that meeting. He was frequently away from home.

Bones also began investing in real estate. He purchased three lots in Miller Heights, north of the railroad tracks and west of the Flats, where no one yet lived. He bought them from an old friend, W. H. Fuqua, for $1,000. Contrary to the old myth that white people gave him things, Bones paid $100 every three months at 10 percent interest. Bones was the first black person in Amarillo to purchase property outside of the Flats. And according to him, he was the first black to make a permanent home in Amarillo, which he did in 1900. Brother Jerry Calloway was living in Amarillo as early as 1895 but as a domestic in the J. C. Callaway home.

Meanwhile, Bones had moved to the Flats, where his wife and stepdaughter had already been living, and for the first time in almost fifty years he was living among his own people. In doing so, he witnessed the real plight of blacks. It may have been here that he came to this conclusion:

I have tried to be Indian and I have tried to be white. I got a strain of white blood in me, but my skin is colored. Now I'm reconciled and satisfied to be colored. . . . I ain't ashamed of my color anymore. Now I'm satisfied to be what God made me, but I'll always see white and think white.[16]

Perhaps it was this reality that was going to work for him and his people in a way no one dreamed. He would use the talents he was born with and friendships he established over the years to get some of the good things in life for his people, himself, and his friends. Within just a few years he would be known more as a civic and social leader than a legendary bronc rider. Because of the cowboy and pioneer reunions, people were not going to forget that he had been one of the best bronc busters of the Plains, but he would carve out a new, even prouder, reputation for himself. He would be known as a leader of his people, a homespun Western philosopher, a humanitarian, a peacemaker, and one who gave honor to whom honor was due without regard to one's race, sex, or creed.

CHAPTER 5

A Negro Town Out on the Prairie: The North Heights Story

Some colored people are envious of my position among white people. They doubt me; they are not in accord with me. They follow me because they know I can get help from the white people, but they do not trust me. Someday, they will understand me.

—Bones Hooks

During the 1920s, the Flats became too crowded, but it was a tight-knit neighborhood, with the Mt. Zion Missionary Baptist Church and the Carter's Chapel A.M.E. Church as its heart and soul. The district's many capable leaders included Phillip and Lanoria Shorten, Max McPayne, and Frank Martin. Then there was Bones Hooks at the age of fifty-eight, being referred to as "Old Bones" by the pioneers.

Many Flats residents were creative and self-sufficient in operating rooming houses, cafes, and shine parlors, but the majority worked as domestics in the homes of the affluent or for the hotels, railroads, and various businesses. The railroads were the largest employer of blacks in the area, with at least four railroads operating out of Amarillo. Amarillo had grown substantially, from about fifteen thousand residents in 1920 to approximately forty-three thousand in 1930, and the black population soared from about three hundred to over sixteen hundred.[1] Amarillo may have anticipated significant growth due to the big land sale, but it was not prepared for such an influx of blacks. The Flats was insufficient to house the majority of the black population, and the servant quarters in the affluent section remained crowded also. Blacks were not permitted to live south of West Third Avenue and were not wanted north of the tracks, though a few black railroad workers lived in areas along the tracks on railroad property that was isolated from residential neighborhoods. In addition to these conditions, blacks were arriving almost daily in Amarillo because there was work to be found.[2]

Amarillo was the major town on the High Plains, even the "Queen City," for it was the cattle and banking business center of the region and an important stopover between St. Louis and California as well as Fort Worth and Denver. Amarillo would also become the Panhandle's business center for energy, as a major oil strike was made in nearby Borger, and the natural-gas fields close to Amarillo were some of the largest in the world.

Amarillo had lots to offer, indeed, but the plight of blacks was growing worse and the gulf between blacks and whites widened. Bones Hooks had property in Miller Heights that remained undeveloped, and it was not enough land to promote a new town site, which he desperately wanted to do. At the age of fifty-eight, Bones had not realized his lifelong dream of creating an "exclusive Negro town." What he did see was the growing prejudice, the passing away of more and more of the pioneers, the lack of housing and healthcare for his people (privileges that he had), and undignified burials. It deeply bothered Bones that when a white died the body got a police escort, but when a black died there was no such respect. Bones, of course, was not subjected to much racism in the Panhandle, but what good was that when his people were so oppressed? He was not happy with the conditions and could not enjoy his personal privileges.

The recent happenings reinforced his dream to build an "exclusive Negro town," and he had not forgotten such towns as Mobeetie, Memphis, and others that openly opposed blacks. Some of them had signs that read similar to this: *Negro Don't Let The Sun Set On You Here!*[3]

That dream was now a burning desire that he couldn't get rid of; it consumed him. Bones Hooks, the great bronc rider, pioneer, legend, and friend to many, knew that with his influence among the whites he could accomplish things that others of his race maybe could not. However, he was not blinded by self-importance, for he recognized the obstacles in his way. Years earlier, blacks had tried to build a church on the north side of the tracks, but the movement was broken. Another place on that side of town, the Brown Mattress Factory, had been a meeting place for the early black Christians, but that mysteriously burned down, and when they built an arbor in which to worship, cowboys destroyed that.[4] They were forced to stay in their own neighborhood, and after dark, those who lived in the servant quarters of the well-to-do kept an extremely low profile. Whites didn't want them running about after dark and didn't want them spreading to other parts of the city. They had their own neighborhood, didn't they? It was the Flats, that section down by the tracks with the constant banging of the railcars, in the area that was no longer desirable to whites.

Bones, on the other hand, had never kept a low profile anywhere that he had lived and wasn't about to do it now. He moved quickly in the spring of 1926 as lots were being sold to blacks and others in East Amarillo in the Mirror Addition not far from the stockyards. The land developer was Angus ("A. P.") McSwain, but there was another landowner in the same area, Lee Bivins, who was a pioneer and old friend of Bones. Bivins was a wealthy humanitarian and civic and social leader, and by the mid-1920s, he was considered the largest landowner in the West and the biggest individual rancher in regards to the number of cattle he annually shipped to market. In addition, he was the mayor of Amarillo in 1926, after serving several years on the City Commission. During the summer of 1926, Bones purchased four lots from Bivins. The Scottish developer, McSwain, had purchased about thirty-five lots from Bivins, some as early as 1924, and was also selling to blacks. McSwain was the only real-estate man willing to sell property outside the Flats to blacks.[5]

Obstacles and Opportunities

The proposed addition looked to have much promise, but immediately proved otherwise. The nearby residents didn't want blacks putting up houses on these lots, and the cowboys harassed and drove out those who had purchased lots, including Bones. If a new neighborhood had been started in this area, it would have had the same problem as the Flats—it did not have much room to expand, due to a large Mexican population that had been there for about twenty years. In fact, the Mexicans there outnumbered blacks then as they do now. As for the cowboys who opposed the blacks' presence, they were of another generation, young and white, and did not give Bones the respect that he deserved and had earned. The proposed addition was a disgrace. This was not what Bones had envisioned, to say the least. He realized more than ever that his people needed land away from the whites so that they might live out their lives in the way that they wished. Yet it needed to be close enough to downtown that they were easily able to get to work and back.

The first venture was a total bust, not only to Bones but McSwain as well. Yet Bones was not deterred. He had pioneered this land when it was only prairie with head-tall grass,

Lee Bivins, as mayor of Amarillo. *Courtesy of the Amarillo Downtown Library.*

and such things as electricity and automobiles were not even imagined. He had taken a step backwards, but he would soon prove just how resourceful he could be.

He didn't have to wait long, as another opportunity arrived just a couple of months later. One hundred and five acres of desirable land was for sale north and west of town. Part of this land had originally been platted for the Texas State Normal Teachers College (later West Texas A&M), but instead the school decided to locate to Canyon, south of Amarillo. This land was certainly attractive for many reasons, but what Bones liked best about it was that it was far enough away from the whites that the black residents could live undisturbed and close enough to town that they could easily get to their jobs.

The owners were J. O. and Maude Whittington and the price was $25,000 with a down payment of $8,500. Bones knew this land well. He had long referred to it as the Heights because it was higher than downtown Amarillo and not vulnerable to flooding waters from Wild Horse Lake. Bones had camped here in the pioneer days on trail drives to and from the cattle markets in Kansas. The land had sentimental value for him and he was determined to build his town on this site.[6]

While Bones was naturally excited about the prospect, he was equally cautious. He had the recent debacle as a reminder and wasn't about to rush in and make the same mistakes. He also had concerns about buying the land outright, not just because of the failure in East Amarillo but for deep personal reasons.

Bones had been associating with affluent whites, pioneer ranchers, and cattlemen for years and had been called by some the "whitest black man" in Texas due to his unique relationship with whites. He feared that if he bought the land outright and sold it to his people, many would think he was trying to make money off them like the white man and would resent him for it.

Bones wasn't interested in making money for himself, but he did want the black community to prosper and he did want to build an "exclusive Negro town." Obviously, he needed help in order to do it. He needed the white man's help. Going to his white friends would not change his image as the "whitest black man," but he had little choice. He needed some real backing, so he went to his old friend, Lee Bivins.

Bivins had proved that he was philanthropic. He also relied on another's word and often sealed important deals with nothing more than a firm handshake. He had donated money and property all over town and would be a generous benefactor to the black community before his untimely death.

Bones marched right into Bivins' office, trampling down race barriers, and asked to see the mayor. Certainly, no other black person could do this in those times. Bivins cordially received him, as usual. Bones explained his vision of an "exclusive Negro town," as he probably had on a previous occasion. When he finished, he asked Bivins to purchase the property and sell it to his people at reasonable prices. Bivins was an inquiring man and wanted to know why Bones didn't just buy it outright. He knew Bones had the money. Bones answered, "If I do, my people will think I'm trying to make money off them. If you do it, they'll think it's something big." Bivins promised to help, and they shook hands on it.[7]

Getting Bivins' help was one thing, but Bones knew he still had much to do on his end. One of his biggest obstacles was to convince his people to move out to the undeveloped prairie, where there was no electricity, water, gas, or transportation, and pioneer the land. Another problem was going to be opposition from certain whites. Then there were those of his own race who did not trust him because of his unusual relationship with whites and his attendance at the annual cowboy, pioneer, and settler reunions. Yet he and his people knew that he was in a better position than anyone else to help them. Perhaps this was the moment that everything in his past had prepared him for, and if so, he was ready for the challenge.

Bones undoubtedly grasped that in order to get some of the good things in life that the whites took for granted, he needed the whites' help. Blacks had no voice in the predominantly white Panhandle, except for Bones. They were far from any center of black population, and their increasing numbers in the isolated Panhandle meant increasing prejudice. Bones may have been living a double standard, the same double standard he had always despised, but he was willing to walk that tightrope in order to help his people.

In doing so, Bones said some blacks "doubted" him and were not "in accord" with him, but someday they would "understand" him. Bones had often expressed in the past that he thought white and saw white but had accepted his skin color and was glad to be black. Other times, he seemed white to whites and black to blacks. Bones was either the most mysterious man in Amarillo or the most clever. He seemed to belong to two races but was at home with neither. He was surely an enigma to all who knew him.

As Bones conferred with Bivins about the proposed Heights, A. P. McSwain, the land developer, entered the picture once again. On September 7, 1926, he purchased 100 of the 105 acres that were for sale by the Whittingtons and created the North Heights Land Company. The section was platted as the North Heights Addition, as it had always been known, and he intended to sell exclusively to blacks.[8]

The Mayor Supports Bones

As previously noted, the Panhandle real-estate companies had not been kind to blacks, but McSwain didn't seem averse to meeting blacks' needs for additional housing while simultaneously seeing a profit. Following his initial purchase of the land, results were swift. Just twenty-two days after the plat of the North Heights, on September 29, the City Commissioners approved the "Negro Addition" and said that the date of the sale of lots would be announced later. However, McSwain already had an opening-day sale on September 15, two weeks prior to the commissioners' approval of the sale. This seems to point to some sort of missed communication between McSwain and the city officials.

Perhaps it was not a miscommunication at all. Lee Bivins was not promoting McSwain's North Heights, but Bones' holdings there. Bones' property covered the five acres that McSwain had been unable to purchase and that had been owned by Bivins, who was exclusively promoting Bones' venture. It appears that the City Commissioners had approved Bones' lots for sale on the twenty-ninth of September.

These were certainly two different developments in the North Heights. McSwain had the larger one, of course, originally covering eight square blocks, Twenty-second Avenue south to Fifteenth Avenue and Jefferson Street west to Ong Street. Bones' section was small by comparison, at the southernmost end of the North Heights, encompassing the entire block of Adams Street from Fifteenth to Sixteenth avenues.[9]

McSwain's opening-day sale of the North Heights had been successful, with sales totaling more than thirteen thousand dollars. Excitement ran wild and there was praise throughout the city for the new addition. But the enthusiasm soon faded. Sales and monthly payments fell off as initial landowners had a change of heart. Some demanded their money back and others just quit making payments. This was through no fault of McSwain, who sold the lots cheaply and offered a simple payment plan. Furthermore, he was willing to accommodate prospective buyers, meeting them in the Flats if they wished even though he kept an office in downtown Amarillo.[10]

McSwain later moved a shack to the corner of Hughes

and Twelfth Avenue that served as the North Heights Land Company office and temporary housing for him and his family. He moved a house opposite the corner of the real-estate office the following year where he, his wife, Edith, and their two sons lived.[11]

Throughout the history of the North Heights, Bones never drew a distinction between his section and McSwain's. He was never involved in any kind of petty competition in the Heights. Both sections were equally opposed. McSwain's and Bones' objective was the same—to establish a black neighborhood. Of course, their reasons were different, but the goal was the same. Surprisingly, little opposition came from the affluent white section south of the tracks on Polk, Taylor, Tyler, and Pierce streets, where lived the Bivinses, Fuquas, Wares, Eakles, and other prominent Amarilloans. In fact, they were delighted that the North Heights had been established, but their support was selfish rather than fair. The servant quarters in their section had long been overcrowded, and many who lived there did not work on the premises. It was a touchy problem, and the North Heights appeared to be the solution.

Still, there was some strong opposition from the white sector. The all-white North Amarillo Civic Club (NACC) wanted to develop and beautify North Amarillo, which was due north of downtown Amarillo across the tracks. Rev. G. H. Bryant, of the Buchanan Street Methodist Church, led this organization. Their biggest concern about the North Heights was that its residents had to pass through North Amarillo to get to and from work in downtown Amarillo. They also proposed that the white Presbyterian Children's Home would have to relocate due to the proximity of blacks.[12]

The Opposition

This was not the first time that whites had opposed the expansion of the black community nor the first time that the

NACC had done so. As early as 1912 they opposed the proposed construction of a black church on the north side of the tracks, because no blacks lived on that side and therefore, they reasoned, ought not to have a church there.[13] Yet a few blacks did live there, on property probably owned by the Fort Worth & Denver Railroad. This was about the same time that the Brown Mattress Factory burned down.

The NACC made its formal protests against the North Heights on March 22, 1927, at the City Commissioners meeting. Lee Bivins was absent, but it didn't matter. The NACC's efforts were for naught, for the commissioners handed down a final and absolute verdict. They announced that the "Negro Addition" would stand: "The matter has been solved and permanently settled satisfactory to all concerned."[14] If the NACC had won, there would surely have been an uproar from Bivins and his wealthy neighbors, but it didn't come to that.

The NACC was the least of Bones' problems, however. The prairie land where he wanted his people to live had none of the conveniences they were used to: gas, electricity, and water, not to mention trolley-car service to the addition, as most could not afford cars. Perhaps such sacrifices were too high. They were not pioneers and had arrived in Amarillo after it was already modernized. On the other hand, Bones realized that no one was born a pioneer but became one out of necessity. He knew that these newcomers would be able to pioneer the Heights the same way he and others had pioneered the Panhandle some forty years before.

Bones understood that he had to lead the way, set the example, and he was already doing that. Besides the investment he had made in the fifteenth block of Adams Street, he had purchased undeveloped property west of the Flats on Jefferson Street and was the new owner of the Corner Drug Store in the Flats. He also purchased additional lots from McSwain in the Heights and moved a house to one of the lots. A two-story building erected at 1511 Adams Street would be Bones' most impressive investment. It cost $14,000, with a $750 down payment and monthly payments of $150.[15] Bones' real-estate holdings were already impressive, but his finances would still be tied up for years in order to make his dream come true. He would not be rich in money but in the friendships he made over the years. These friendships would aid him as he promoted and firmly established the Heights.

One might easily believe that Bones and McSwain were partners in the Heights, but that is not true. However, neither were they staunch competitors. McSwain needed Bones more than Bones needed him, even though McSwain held the larger property. Bones was the one with charisma who could tirelessly promote the North Heights.

According to H. V. McSwain, A. P. McSwain's son, Bivins partially financed McSwain, but a closer look reveals that Bivins exclusively financed Bones Hooks. It appears that McSwain cashed in on an insurance policy. The deed points out that the 100 acres he purchased from the Whittingtons were transferred to the Union Standard Life Insurance Company of Dallas.[16] They were not mortgaged by Lee Bivins, as many have believed.

Pioneer Hall

The two-story building on Adams Street, which Bones had purchased from Bivins during the summer of 1927, would have a colorful and important history. It would become the civic and social center of the North Heights. Bones had originally hoped it would be a hospital for his people. However, at the time there was no black physician in Amarillo, and Bones indicated that if there had been, the physician would have been reluctant to go out to the undeveloped Heights. There was no public transportation, and black doctors were too poor to own automobiles.

The building was destined for another use. Bones named it Pioneer Hall, and he, Minnie, and Georgia moved into the building in July 1927. He opened up a small grocery store on the ground floor, the upstairs was rented out to those building homes nearby, and he rented other spaces to organizations such as the Colored Masons and the Negro Chamber of Commerce. They also held barbecues and weekend dances to offset expenses. With Bones' presence in the Heights, others were encouraged to buy into the dream of an "exclusive Negro town."[17]

Not surprisingly, home construction soon centered on the southern edge of the Heights around Pioneer Hall. Even more interestingly, the North Heights Land Company office was located south of Bones' property, in Miller Heights. The population growth started around Bones' Pioneer Hall and then moved south into Miller Heights. It would be many years before the McSwain section was fully developed.

Bones was unequivocally the leader of his people in Amarillo, and his achievement was known all over the Panhandle. Although there were strong church leaders in the Flats, no one commanded the respect that he did. Bones was a quiet but determined man, and he explained one of the reasons behind his dream: "I wanted our people to have an exclusive town and show the white man we could live as decent law abiding citizens so that when a black man committed a crime that the white man couldn't say all darkies were alike."[18]

Bones once stated that he wouldn't let any whites into his town, yet he was the first to admit that he couldn't have built it alone. He needed help from whites, especially Lee Bivins, to whom he gave considerable credit, not just for his financial support but also for bringing modernization to the North Heights through his influence in city government. Bivins used his political power to have the Heights annexed

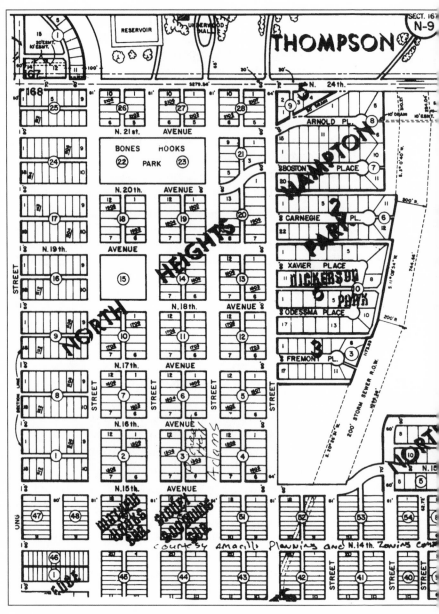

Plat of the North Heights and Miller Heights. *Courtesy of the Planning, Zoning and Development Commission of the City of Amarillo.*

to the city of Amarillo and saw to it that water, gas, electricity, and trolley-car service extended to it. This was the result of Bones' promotion and work. McSwain's Heights could not have succeeded without Bones' participation, and not just participation, but leadership. Bones had the will to make it all happen and the spirit of a true pioneer.

In retrospect, one can see how all of the pieces fell into place. Of course, one of those pieces was Bones' friendship with Lee Bivins and all of the other pioneers. Bivins threw his support behind Bones because he believed in the man. A mutual respect bound all of the pioneers together. And A. P. McSwain's part in the development cannot be overlooked, because he was willing to sell to blacks when most white real-estate men were not. He negotiated on their own terms and hired blacks to assist him, among those being James Driver in the early stages and Clifford Austin later on. W. H. Fuqua, the president of the First National Bank, also supported Bones' dream and had several business dealings with him.

But Bones was the backbone of the Heights. He had a vision of a place where his people might live without being under the constant scrutiny of the whites. With daring leadership he heavily invested into his dream and into Pioneer Hall. He pushed ahead while many were unsure of the future of the Heights.

Through it all, Bones was never an agent for McSwain or anyone else. But he was the best agent and promoter McSwain and the Heights ever had—and he didn't even get a commission. Neither was he in a position to profit from his real-estate holdings, as nearly everything he had saved over the years was tied up, and the credit he received was solely on his word, his handshake, and his good name. Nevertheless, Bones got something far better than monetary rewards. He realized a lifelong dream. But from his own point of view, this would not be his greatest accomplishment.

That was still to come.

CHAPTER 6

The Man of the People and the Unofficial Mayor of the Heights

If I want to help my people, I must remain with them.
—Bones Hooks

Bones tirelessly hit home his message:

This country has grown from a wilderness just because
white people sacrificed and worked early and late. They
didn't sit down for someone to give them something. They
went after it themselves. That's what you've got to do.

But he did more than preach the "exclusive Negro town."
He was busy developing it further. He purchased additional
property from Bivins and McSwain. Some of it was adjacent
south of his Adams Street holdings and became the Bones
Hooks Subdivision; he also purchased some of the Lowery
Estate when it was sold off. His holdings were quite impressive for an old cowboy, but all of it would finance the
Heights and his other projects for years to come. Bones
proudly proclaimed, "We have sixty-five families living here
and everyone owns a home."[1] He had every right to boast.

The Heights enjoyed a celebrated status as the most
impressive black community in the Panhandle, with the
brick Pioneer Hall being the center of its social and civic

119

life. However, it was not the only black community in the Panhandle. Clarendon claimed the oldest one in the Panhandle, as the one in Mobeetie was all but gone due in a great part to the closing of Fort Elliott in 1890. Memphis had started a black community in 1922, about ten years after the Flats was established. Even so, Memphis had a reputation for being unfriendly towards blacks. It was rumored that when a train arrived at the Memphis depot, the porters refused to get off. Unlike in Amarillo, blacks first arrived in Memphis shortly before 1920 and quite possibly as early as 1917 to pick cotton. As their numbers grew, the whites wanted to keep an eye on them; thus they created the Morningside Addition.[2]

About the same time that Bones was developing the Heights, there was a black population boom and black communities were established all over the Panhandle. The newest ones were in counties where cotton had become a major crop, below the Caprock in Childress in Childress County and Wellington in Collingsworth County. Because of the cotton, the little community in Clarendon in Donley County grew even larger. Above the Caprock and closer to Amarillo were Pampa in Gray County and Borger in Hutchinson County. The growth of these two towns was directly related to the discovery of oil and gas in the area. After the discovery of oil in Borger in 1926, the population swelled from a few to over ten thousand in just a few months. But it would never replace Amarillo as the major town in the Panhandle. An older town, Panhandle City, which at one time was expected to benefit greatly from the railroads and the oil and gas discoveries, was to remain small, and a black community never developed there as it did in these other places.[3]

During the Heights' prosperous times in the late 1920s, race problems arose in other parts of the Panhandle. In Alanreed in southern Gray County in 1927, Frank

Weatherby, his wife, and children were slain in their home. The suspects were believed to have been black. The murder weapon, a handgun, was traced to a local black man who had sold it to someone else and he was cleared. However, the murders set off an anti-black sentiment that had already been simmering. Some whites ordered Alanreed blacks to leave their homes or face armed vigilantes. The sheriff from Amarillo was sent to investigate. The whites initiated the first race riots in the Panhandle, which spread from Alanreed to Hedley, Shamrock, and Wellington, covering parts of three counties. Fortunately the situation did not escalate further.[4]

More trouble started in Childress shortly after the Weatherby incident when fights broke out between whites and blacks in a downtown alley. Several other fights followed, and certain whites decided that every black should be run out of town. They went to the servant houses, where most of the blacks lived, and ordered them to leave, threatening harm if they didn't. This trouble may have resulted partly from the Weatherby murders, but a more direct provocation was that blacks were building homes in a white section of town.[5]

A couple of years later, and much farther north in the oil-boom town of Borger, a similar incident occurred. Borger was just about to undergo its darkest hour as organized crime ran rampant. Corruption controlled the mayor's and sheriff's offices, and the district attorney was assassinated. The governor imposed martial law and summoned the Texas Rangers and state militia to restore order. Following on the heels of this lawlessness, blacks of Borger were trying to establish a neighborhood of their own when a black family's home was bombed. This was certainly an act of severe intimidation against the fifty black families moving near the railroad tracks in the northeast part of town. John Smith had founded the original black section in the northwest part of town, but the community had outgrown that. Smith was an associate of the town's shady character, Ace Borger, but proved to be a generous and resourceful man to his people. The new section consisted of four blocks of property that had been sold to blacks, who were building homes on these lots. The trouble was that they were building adjacent to three houses of whites. Despite the opposition, this became the permanent black section.[6]

While race problems were a growing concern in other parts of the Panhandle, the North Heights Addition of Amarillo was flourishing. Much of the credit must go to Bones. If he had been determined to build in the Mirror Addition in East Amarillo, he might have been opposed not only by the whites but the Mexicans, too. His failure in East Amarillo proved fortunate, as the Heights was an area where his people could greatly expand their boundaries.

At this time, a former leader returned to Amarillo for special work. He was Rev. Miles Jenkins, the visionary and missionary who organized and established the Mt. Zion Missionary Baptist Church with the assistance of very capable Christians. This time he was in town to establish another church and it was going to be in the North Heights. It became known as the Jenkins Chapel.

Jenkins organized the church in the spring of 1926, but it had no home yet. Lots in the Heights were not sold until September. Jenkins purchased a building at that time for $300, and within three years, working tirelessly as ever, he paid off the first mortgage. The Jenkins Chapel was considered the most attractive building in the Heights, being constructed of brick with pews and the pulpit made of oak. The stained-glass windows were a gift from Bones, who asked for them from his friends at the Polk Street Methodist Church, which had replaced them with new ones.[7]

In the same year another minister, Rev. J. L. Langston, arrived in Amarillo and established a new denomination in the Flats, which was now growing westwards. He was not a Baptist like Jenkins but a member of the Holiness Church, otherwise known as the Church of God in Christ. He was a young, unmarried minister, and someone thought he ought to meet the community's most distinguished citizen, Bones Hooks. Years later, Langston reflected on his association with Bones:

> Bones was the man who sold me on the idea of remaining in West Texas. He knew the West and impressed me to remain. He introduced me to each of the bank presidents; First National, Amarillo National and American National. He made me feel the people in the West had the utmost confidence in him which I soon realized.[8]

Langston must have been truly amazed when Bones marched him into the banks and asked to see the presidents. He was probably even more astonished when they were received. This was practically unheard of in any town in the heavily segregated U.S., but Bones was no ordinary citizen. He was a favored son and virtually had the keys to the city.

So Langston stayed in Amarillo, built his church, and became a fast and faithful friend to Bones. Langston also made a reputation for himself as an active leader and worked hard to alleviate some of the problems of the poor. One of his projects was the opening of a soup kitchen in the Flats, and he fed all who were hungry, regardless of color. He and Bones had similar visions. Langston was Bones' most trusted confidant, but he could never get Bones to formally join his congregation. Bones, the son of a Baptist preacher, never joined any church but supported them all. He understood how important they were to a community. Still, he was intrigued by Langston's denomination.

Negro School Is Organized

While Langston was building his church piece by piece,

Bones labored equally hard to establish a high school in the North Heights. He led a delegation that submitted a request to the school officials, and he received a reply on February 24, 1928. It read:

> Dear Mathew:
>
> At the School Board meeting last night your petition was submitted, and the Board instructed me to write you that they have under consideration of establishing a school for your people in the North Heights Addition, and have made an offer for a site that was refused. The Board feels that they have offered as much as they should for a site that far out, and this is as far as they can go toward establishing a school until a suitable site is secured.
>
> Yours very truly,
> Geo. M. Waddill.
> Secretary.[9]

The search continued and a suitable site was found. Patten High, the first black high school in the Panhandle, was established in the Heights and named after its principal, Prof. S. C. Patten. He had previously been the principal at the Fred Douglass Elementary School in the Flats. He served as principal at Patten High from 1929 until 1947, when a new high school was erected. Patten believed in Bones' dream and, like many others, thought that a segregated community was best for their people at this time. Patten was more than a teacher. Like many of Bones' closest friends, he was a minister, belonging to the African Methodist Episcopal (A.M.E.) Church.

The A.M.E. was established in 1927, and as with most of the early churches, its meetings began in the members' homes. The church permanently located to the Heights on property generously donated by Lee Bivins. It was originally referred to as the Patten Chapel, and Rev. S. C. Patten was its first pastor. But his tenure was brief, lasting from 1927 to 1929, and after the church was accepted into the Northwest Texas Conference it became St. John's A.M.E. Church. Patten would always be willing to serve in any capacity necessary, and in 1933 he was again called to lead the congregation. He served this time only until 1934, when another successor was found.[10]

The Heights had grown by leaps and bounds by 1930, but there were still numerous vacant lots, particularly in McSwain's section between North Twenty-second and North Eighteenth avenues, because the most growth occurred near Pioneer Hall on North Fifteenth Avenue. Houses were on lots all around Pioneer Hall and even southwards into Miller Heights, where the Mathew Hooks Subdivision was soon established. The Sidney Goodwin and Clarence Watley subdivisions would be established near Bones' property a little later.

Things looked very bright for the Heights. Then Lee Bivins suddenly died on January 18, 1929, of heart failure in Wichita Falls, Texas, while in that city on business. Whites and blacks alike lost a friend and benefactor. He would be sorely missed. Bones paid his respects to the Bivins family by presenting them with the guerdon of honor, the single white flower, his tradition that was well known and received with heartfelt gratitude. Lee Bivins would not be the last of this pioneer family to whom Bones would pay tribute.

With the death of Lee Bivins, Bones lost a powerful friend and ally. Bivins was succeeded as mayor by an up-and-coming young businessman and a hero in World War I, Col. Ernest O. Thompson. Thompson was not a pioneer in the same sense as Bones and Bivins, but he was the same caliber of man. He first came to Amarillo in 1902 with his family at the age of ten. Following his graduation from Amarillo High School, he attended the Virginia Military Institute and the University of Texas, where he earned a law degree. He entered the army and served in World War I, where he achieved the rank of lieutenant colonel as a result of heroism in battle under Gen. John J. Pershing. He remained in Europe after the war, was placed in charge of Germany's military arms with the occupation army, and helped organize the American Legion.[11]

Once Thompson came home, he set up a successful law practice and purchased the Amarillo Hotel from H. P. Canode. Then he built a new Amarillo Hotel and married international Metropolitan Opera star May Peterson. As mayor, he mandated a major civic-improvement campaign. He later purchased the Herring Hotel, Amarillo's first multistoried hotel. In 1932 he filled a vacant position on the powerful Railroad Commission, where he became known as the "Fighting Mayor" and "Fighting Red Thompson" for opposing the "hot oil" operators of East Texas, who were defying the state's authority.[12]

But long before Thompson was a war hero and the "Fighting Mayor," Bones knew him as a boy. Years after his bronc-riding days were over, Bones was still in demand to teach affluent white boys to ride horses. Most boys had dreams of being cowboys, but two particular young boys seemed different from the rest. Bones remembered them quite well—Ernest O. Thompson and Earl Fuqua, the son of his old friend, bank president W. H. Fuqua. Bones recalled:

> Years ago I taught Col. Ernest Thompson and Earl Fuqua to ride. They didn't seem enthusiastic about it as some of the other boys and I did not know what to think about them. This was cow country then and I wanted all the boys to be cowpunchers, but I can see it all now. Colonel Thompson had to develop into a big businessman and our mayor and Mr. Fuqua into a banker. That's what we need them for.[13]

Thompson and Fuqua indeed helped lead Amarillo into

the modern age, for which they received their due credit. Bones was doing the same thing in the Heights, but he remained a cowboy at heart, and his language was often littered with words and phrases that were familiar to the old pioneers. Concerning the Heights, Bones said, "I have pitched camp for the last time, I have made down my bed and located the chuck wagon and I want everybody to help make our new range the best in the country."[14]

In 1929, the stock market crashed, a noise heard around the world, and the depression soon followed. But Bones had high hopes of better things to come. He boasted:

> We're building a $15,000 church and we have a fine school building. We have a civic center in a two-story brick building [Pioneer Hall] and this Negro boy's dream has come true for we have a real place to have all of our meetings, socials, etc. We want the white folks to come out and see what we are doing and have done, and we know that the people of Amarillo are going to do great things in the next few years.[15]

What exactly were they doing in the Heights? Bones was among those who organized the "Negro Chamber of Commerce," which met at Pioneer Hall, as did the "Colored Masons." The leader of the chamber movement was a Heights homeowner, Flynn Williams, and it had over sixty original members. Frank Smiley was president; C. Watson was first vice-president; Raymond Hudson was second vice-president; Doc Gray was third vice-president and treasurer. Among the listed members were Bones Hooks, Rev. J. L. Langston, Prof. S. C. Patten, Sidney Goodwin, and Rev. Miles Jenkins.[16]

The organization's purpose was to "promote the welfare of Amarillo Negroes, assist them in finding employment and cooperate with the development and beautification of Amarillo." It would also be influential in mediating some of the problems between blacks and whites in elections for public officials. A breakdown in voting rights had occurred in 1928, when it was announced that blacks would not be allowed to vote in the elections. Grover B. Hill, the Democratic county chairman, had said, "I am at a loss to understand why any candidate would insist upon allowing Negroes to vote in a white man's primary, or would ask Negroes to vote for him when none of them would vote for a Negro."[17]

Bones was not outspoken on the subject, but as always he worked quietly behind the scenes to get things changed. However, it was going to take more than his influence to break down these barriers, and some others tried. In 1932 Ernest Fielder, an Amarillo resident since 1909, led a delegation of ten who tried to vote, but they were turned down. A few Texas counties abolished the old carpetbagger rule and permitted blacks to cast votes in the Democratic primary, but no black votes were cast in the Panhandle.[18]

The discrimination of the times took a back seat to the stock market crash of 1929, and Amarillo was affected as much as anywhere else. It was, of course, followed by the depression and a decade of dust storms as never seen before on the Plains. During these times few blacks had money in any of the banks. They had few possessions to lose and no security whatsoever. Not much changed for them in those days. Rev. Jess Cortez, a black native of Amarillo, said that blacks couldn't get bank loans or good jobs before 1929 anyway.

Yet blacks were certainly affected. For instance, when businesses, ranches, and farms folded or went deep into debt, blacks were put out of work. Some of the affluent whites were not so well-to-do all of a sudden and couldn't afford some of their former luxuries nor their servants, or at least not all of their domestic help. Things that were scarce in the first place practically disappeared, as economic belts were tightened and the Heights' growth was curtailed. During this decade of the depression, Bones was very generous to his people.

The 1920s had so far been Amarillo's greatest decade of growth, but this slowed significantly during the 1930s. Other cities and counties even regressed. But this would not happen right away. Jobs remained in Amarillo in the early 1930s because of the powerful railroads; the oil, gas, cattle, and wheat industries; and the large number of wealthy families there who continued to put money into the economy.[19]

Nevertheless, the decade proved to be a major crossroads for Bones, with some personal failures and new accomplishments. Minnie Bishop and Bones were divorced in September of 1930. It had been a difficult marriage that had not suited either party very well. He was away from the family most of the time, speaking at functions, raising money for his projects, going to the cowboy, pioneer, and old settlers' reunions, and continually promoting the Heights as well as the entire Panhandle.[20] This contributed to his terrible relationship with his stepdaughter, Georgia. According to her, Bones was "a mean old man" who "was always fighting" with her mother, and to this day Georgia (Mrs. Wendell Faulks) has only bad memories of her childhood in the Hooks home in the North Heights.

In 1930 Bones retired from the Santa Fe Railroad with a pension, a gold watch, and a lifetime pass on the railway for his twenty-one years of good service. But his retirement was not entirely voluntary, as he was injured in his dangerous job as Pullman. Georgia Faulks said the injury was a hernia that he was not willing to take care of through surgery.[21]

Meanwhile, there was no indication that a depression had begun in Amarillo, as the city saw a sort of building boom. In addition to the construction in the private sector, the roads were being improved, schools were being remodeled, and new schools were springing up under the Thompson administration. The Fred Douglass School in the Flats had a major facelift in which improvements and investments in tile and stucco came to $6,500. However, during the same period, the costs at the white schools were staggering. For example, the Sam Houston School received $289,202 worth of brick, Forrest Hill $208,567 worth of brick, and Lee Bivins School $183,025 worth of brick and tile. The public-school system obviously benefited from a healthy local economy. It also indicated how little of the wealth was being distributed to the black community.[22]

About this time, the pioneers were getting together with the historical society to organize a museum that would honor both groups. Bones and his white friends met in Canyon, Texas, at the pioneer campground at West Texas Teachers College, to discuss raising money for the museum's construction. Bones was sixty-two and the only black member of the historical society. He had plenty to say at the meeting. Some of his words were preserved for later generations:

> These men and women came to the Panhandle country when it was almost a desert and the only thing they brought with them was a vision. They stayed on and saw their visions materialize. They were builders and you can look around the Panhandle today and see their results. They found this section just big barren country flattened out here on Earth. But look at it now. The pioneers did it.[23]

Bones Speaks at Historical Society

In August 1930, Bones attended the Cowboy Reunion. In November, he celebrated his birthday with black friends at Pioneer Hall, but he also received best wishes from the white pioneers. In the following spring, he returned to Canyon for the annual meeting of the Panhandle-Plains Historical Society. The meeting was opened before the faculty and approximately a thousand white-faced students. There were morning, afternoon, and evening festivities with speakers throughout the day, including Olive Dixon, the widow of the famous buffalo hunter, army scout, and participant at the Battle of Adobe Walls, Billy Dixon; J. Evetts Haley, the historian and biographer of Charles Goodnight; Mel Armstrong of Old Tascosa; and Judge J. W. Hoover, who was the main speaker of the day.

The most interesting speaker, however, was Bones Hooks. He was even the very first speaker that morning because they wanted a moving and emotional start, and Bones was always eager to talk when the topic was the pioneer days. He was also an expert storyteller in the spirit of the campfire tales and could talk about the old days endlessly. Needless to say, the young white students were surprised, perhaps even shocked, when the dark-skinned cowboy walked up to the podium, for they were not accustomed to blacks sharing the platform with whites. In fact, there was not another black face in sight. But they were not disappointed. Dr. Joseph A. Hill, president of the college at the time and author of the history of the museum, wrote that "Bones gave a rousing speech," the kind the program had wanted. He also wrote, "Old Bones in his half of the century pioneering on the Plains had become part of the history that the historical society was organized to preserve."[24]

Almost at the same time that Bones and his pioneer friends were celebrating history, camping out, and swapping old tales over a barbecue, something was happening back in Amarillo. A black hotel porter named Slim Moore killed Pete ("Mont") Moore, a white cowboy, at the porter's downtown hotel. Slim was silent about his actions at first but later admitted he had shot and killed the cowboy. Then he demanded to represent himself. There were at least three witnesses, the trial was swift, the verdict was guilty, and the porter was sentenced to death. It would have ended there and Slim would have been put to death, but another witness, a white man, came forward with new evidence, and a second trial was ordered. This time Slim declined to represent himself. His testimony was corroborated by the story of the new witness.[25]

The porter had been on duty at the Terminal Hotel not far from the Santa Fe Depot when Mont Moore and his three friends came in. The men all appeared to be drunk and one of them asked about a friend staying at the hotel. The porter couldn't find such a person in the register and the men took it to look for themselves. They cursed and threatened him and hit him over the head with the register. He dodged behind the counter, and when he looked up one of the men was holding a chair over him. He crawled on his knees to escape, but Mont cut him off. Fearing for his life, Slim reached for the pistol in the drawer and shot Mont.[26]

Bill Anderson was the new witness who had seen the killing. It was suggested that he came forward only after being induced to do so with money. The trial got ugly and a fight broke out between Clem C. Calhoun, the special prosecutor, and E. T. ("Dusty") Miller, the defense counsel. After peace was restored, the trial continued and concluded. The jury deliberated three hours and fifteen minutes. When the verdict was read, Slim Moore couldn't believe what he had heard. He didn't think that they'd really let him go free—not a Negro. When it hit him, he ran to the jailhouse and asked the jailer to lock him up, presumably for his own protection. However, Slim Moore was now a free man, and he disappeared into the night.[27]

The jury acquitted Slim Moore in an act of decency in a sensational trial. Perhaps Bones was correct when he said there was always one good person willing to stand up for what was right, even in the meanest mob. Little trouble resulted from the verdict. Maybe it was because Mont Moore was not a local but from Tucumcari, New Mexico. Blacks naturally felt vindicated, but there was something behind the trial that could easily have touched off some gory violence. Slim had been reluctant to talk at his trial, but according to some old-time residents, he had been having a relationship with a white maid who also worked at the Terminal Hotel, and that was why the white cowboys came looking for trouble with him. That knowledge, for the most part, remained a secret within the black community for the peace of all.[28]

As blacks celebrated the verdict, Bones started a new project in the Heights. There was a lot of violence going on in the community, especially in the Flats: stabbings, shootings, street fights, drunken incidents, and other black-on-black problems. A particularly dangerous alley, between Harrison and Van Buren streets, was called "Death Alley." Pastor Cortez suggested later that no outsider could safely venture into "Death Alley." There were other trouble spots, too, and many of the children were without fathers, being raised by mothers, other relatives, or friends. There were few forms of entertainment to keep the children out of trouble. So Bones began entertaining young boys at Pioneer Hall. Yet this was not entirely new. As early as 1928, children were meeting there for events hosted by the North Heights Needlecraft and Art Club. The activities included croquet, baseball, and a literacy program, and the day's festivities would finish with a picnic. The president of the club was the then Mrs. Bones Hooks, who had "always been an active club worker," and the "Needlecraft and Art Club was fortunate in having such a leader."[29]

Minnie Hooks was quite involved in the community, and the community surely missed her after the divorce when she took her daughter and moved to Kansas. But Bones saw the neglect of the children and the need for a youth center in which to have fun. So he took the responsibility squarely upon his shoulders and personally financed the project. By 1932 he was providing horse riding, sports, and camping at

and near Pioneer Hall. He would soon be completely dedicated to the youngsters, as this project gave him more pleasure and pride than anything else he would ever do.

Bones returned to Canyon in the spring of 1933 for the
dedication of the Panhandle-Plains Historical Museum. He
presented the old pioneers with a *V*-shaped bouquet of
white flowers and led a delegation to the festivities. Bones
was very historically minded, to say the least, for over the
years he had been collecting letters, photographs, documents, newspaper articles, and interviews and would continue to do for some time. He had already decided that upon
his death the collection was to go to the Panhandle-Plains
Historical Museum.[30]

Bones Establishes a Pioneer Club

The historical society was not the only historically minded
organization with which Bones would be associated. In 1933
he founded a pioneer organization called the Colored
Panhandle Pioneer Club that mirrored the white pioneer
organization. Bones was proud of what his people had
accomplished in the Panhandle and the way they had pioneered the prairie land of the Heights to make it what it was.
In founding this club, he wanted to highlight the remarkable things that his people had done and have everyone be
proud of them, even the whites, just as he was proud of what
the white pioneers had done.

The first meeting was held at Pioneer Hall (where else?)
on June 8, 1933. Sam Jones was elected president, Sidney
Goodwin vice-president, and Mrs. Drucilla secretary. This
was probably the first instance in the Panhandle of a woman
sitting on the board of a mostly male organization. The pioneer club had more than sixty original members, including
Roy Briscoe, age thirty-six and the first black born in the

Panhandle. In order to be a member, one had to have lived in the Panhandle no less than twenty-five years. In 1933 Bones had been in the Panhandle forty-seven years. Only a handful of white pioneers had been in the Panhandle longer.[31]

The first meeting was a noteworthy affair and the *Amarillo Daily News* publicized it, but in the 1930s, everything Bones did was noteworthy. It seemed that a reporter was always waiting around the corner just to get a quote from him, and quite often they did. Bones has probably been quoted more than any real cowboy in history. So naturally they quoted him after the first annual meeting of the Colored Panhandle Pioneer Club. As was expected, Bones praised the spectacular event in his own colorful, down-home manner:

> Folks, it was some roundup. Those mavericks told their experiences in this country when there wasn't much more than some rattlesnakes and some mighty dust storms. We heard our own quartet, The Panhandle Four. These boys were so low we couldn't get under them and so high we couldn't go over them. . . . About 11:30 p.m., I let them drift in with food and drink and they drifted out one by one to the range. And there wasn't a white face in the bunch.[32]

Bones' choice of words might not be understood by those who didn't know him, but he often compared the races to the types of cattle. The whites were Hereford ("white faces") and blacks were Pole Angus ("black faces"). He used to say:

> The white faces were better rustlers, but the black faces fattened easier. The white faces are better rustlers. They were the pioneers. Negroes are not pioneers. They want things already discovered. But they are more easily satisfied.[33]

While Bones was doing many good things to honor the pioneers and their families of both races, it came to Rev. J.

L. Langston's attention that it was Bones who really ought to be honored. In wanting to see that Bones got his due reward, Langston and J. E. Anderson created the Mathew Hooks Memorial Fund. To explain its purpose, Langston wrote:

> Being associated with Bones for a number of years, I find him an outstanding leader and peacemaker among his own race, who did strive to give honor to whom honor was due, regardless of race, color, or creed. And seeing his spirit, I was moved to do something and prove to him that the citizens of Amarillo and all of the Panhandle were concerned about him. So, we organized a Hooks Memorial Club.

Rev. J. L. Langston was elected president, J. E. Anderson general chairman, and dentist M. P. Hines secretary. Other committee members were Dr. F. D. Ramsey, Prof. G. R. Tomlin, Charles Bland, Mose Taylor, Isaiah Saul, Rev. A. J. Williams, and Rev. Roy Blackwell. "And right away, we started a memorial fund to have under construction a nice piece of work."[34]

The organization went public with a letter to the "Citizenship of this Great Empire of Ours—The Panhandle-Plains of Texas." It reminded the people of the Panhandle of Bones' longevity in the region, his good works, and the thirty-nine years that he had been giving the white flower of honor to "every bereaved family of the old pioneers." The letter also described "his untiring efforts" through which he was able to "blend together a friendly relationship between two races that will stand for future generations to come." It ended with the appeal to all to make contributions and the information that the names and donations were to be published from time to time in the newspapers.[35]

The response was good, with whites and blacks alike contributing to the fund. James A. Bush and Chanslor

Weymouth, who were founding members of the Maverick Club, a boys' club for whites, presented stones to the organization for the construction of the monument. It is difficult to guess what Bones thought of all of this hoopla. When told of the monument, he gave his blessing but asked that the legendary Charles Goodnight's name be inscribed on the cornerstone.[36] Construction began on June 5, 1933, and was to be completed on Juneteenth (June 19, which black Texans celebrated as Emancipation Day). Unfortunately it was not, and what happened remains a mystery. But another monument was completed and dedicated about forty-five years later.

Meanwhile, Bones and friends had established a park in the North Heights that was unofficially known as the Bones Hooks Park. Bones had purchased this land years earlier and now dedicated it to the children of the Heights. The project began in 1930 as Bones and his friends took this undeveloped land, beautified it, and planted trees, each one of which was named after a black child in the Heights. The park had lights and a water fountain by 1933. This was the first park in Amarillo that blacks were able to enjoy whenever they desired. It would be the site of many festive occasions, including Juneteenth celebrations, even to this day. Bones spent many pleasing days at the park just like everyone else. Folks gathered there for baseball, which was immensely popular, as well as other fun and games. Churches also met there for picnics and religious events, and Bones took the boys' club there often throughout the years.

Another organization created in 1933 was the Lobo Club, according to the *The Progress Magazine,* which was published in Frank Martin's Hotel in the Flats. The club's mission was civic, social, educational, moral, economic, and patriotic. It supported the federal and local governments and "Americanism," in addition to advocating understanding between and equality of the races. Priority goals were "bigger and better schools, a higher education ratio, better housing, improved streets in Negro districts, sewerage and better transportation." It is doubtful that many of these goals were achieved in these segregated times, but the Lobo Club was effective in raising funds for specific projects by holding barbecues and dinners that promoted the efforts of black businesses. During its thirty or so years of existence, the club had only two lifetime honorary members, Bones Hooks and Brother Jerry Calloway. Bones' qualifications are obvious. Brother Jerry was considered the first black to permanently live in Amarillo, arriving about 1895 according to local history, but it may have been as early as 1891.[37]

Despite all that was going on in the Heights, the most memorable occasion was when Duke Ellington, "the Aristocrat of Jazz," came to Amarillo. The Heights and the Flats had their own talented artists, such as Lanoria Shorten, also known as the "Nightingale of the West", who was in top demand all over the region in religious circles. Another talent was Dutch Campbell, who made a name for himself in the swing clubs and was especially prominent in the clubs in Borger during its heyday. A number of celebrities visited the city over the years, including Joe Louis, Jackie Robinson, and Louis Armstrong. But nothing compared to the excitement that Duke Ellington brought. Juell Shorten Nutter fondly remembered her childhood experience with him. She was playing in front of the Palace Theater in the Flats on West Second Avenue when Ellington appeared and gave candy to all of the children.[38]

Bones Arranges for Duke Ellington to Play

Bones, no stranger to Ellington, would have the pleasure of his company on several occasions. Ellington was in Amarillo to play a concert for the white folks, but Bones thought blacks ought to have the privilege of seeing him as well, and not from some upper balcony or way in the back where they would hardly see him. No, they should see him up close. So Bones spoke with Ellington and then met with officials at the downtown Paramount Theater on Polk Street. He arranged for Ellington to "perform for an all colored audience" at midnight. There was also an earlier performance at the Mt. Zion Missionary Baptist Church at 6:00 P.M. for the elderly and those who could not make the midnight performance. The news spread all over the black communities in the Panhandle. "Some of the patrons came in big cars; some drove in from other towns. All were bent on having a big time, and they had it," Pastor Cortez recalled. This was the first time any blacks had been inside the beautiful theater.[39]

Bones arranged this for the benefit of his people and not for anything else. He had already been told that he could attend any performance or go into any public place that he wished. But he had decided long ago, "if I want to help my people, I must remain with them." He could enjoy privileges that his people could not, but he now denied himself those pleasures. The only privilege he did not give up was his participation in the pioneer and cowboy reunions.[40]

Duke Ellington must have been amazed by how much respect and influence Bones enjoyed among whites in the West and also by his confidence and the manner in which he conducted himself. While Bones was subjected to little prejudice, Ellington and his entourage were forced to live on two Pullman cars in the Santa Fe yard and had to send out to a local Greek restaurant for their food. The times, of course, did not permit blacks to eat in any public place. Duke Ellington must have wondered about this Bones Hooks who commanded so much respect and authority.

Ellington wasn't the only one astonished by Bones' position. Juell Shorten Nutter reflected on it many years later. She remembered walking down Polk Street as a youth with

her father, and as they passed the Amarillo Hotel, she saw
Bones in the restaurant with the old pioneers drinking coffee, laughing, and reminiscing. She realized at a very young
age that Bones was something rare—special—and he could
do things that other blacks couldn't.[41]

As big things happened in Amarillo and Bones stepped
over race barriers, prejudice was escalating in the region.
The Ku Klux Klan gained a foothold in some parts of the
Panhandle, particularly in the cotton counties. The KKK
scouted Amarillo and Clarendon for recruitments and
marches, but it would never have a strong or lasting presence in the area. Lack of support for the Klan there was
probably due to the Panhandle having no slave history and
to the diverse origins of its people. But that was little conso-
lation as discrimination grew stronger without the influence
of the Klan, and with the passing away of the pioneers it was
just a matter of time before the kind of people whom Bones
openly admired were gone forever.

Amarillo was comparatively a large town now, with over forty-
five thousand residents. Many of the faces were newcomers
who brought with them their pasts, lifestyles, and beliefs.
Numerous accounts reported violence in all sectors of
Amarillo. In the Flats, West Third Avenue was known to be wild
and dangerous, with numbers of saloons that had been established since the end of Prohibition. In addition, prostitution
became prevalent, with young girls suddenly arriving from
parts unknown. West Third Avenue became a busy street that
separated the white section from the black section, and numbers of whites would drive down it honking their car horns at
the prostitutes, earning them a nickname—"honkies."

Poverty and violence grew during the depression, but discrimination was as much responsible for the crimes as was
the depression, as some were crimes of necessity. Rev. Jess
Cortez pointed out that the Flats was the heart and soul of
the business district. He said:

[The businesses were the] livelihood of the black community. They [blacks] couldn't go to a lot of places, couldn't
get hired, couldn't make loans to keep businesses up. But
they did the best they could with what they had. They
weren't able to open up [a lot of] businesses and of
course, they committed a lot of crimes because they
couldn't get just loans, couldn't get just money, so they
had to live the best way they could.[42]

Meanwhile, Bones thought that it was time to formally
organize the boys' club that had been meeting at Pioneer
Hall since 1932. It became the Dogie Club, the youngsters
were called Dogies, and Bones, as the founder and director,
was called the Range Boss. The club was officially organized
in 1934 and its organizational meeting was held at the Mt.
Zion Missionary Baptist Church on July 13, 1934. Emmett
Galloway, one of the founders of the Maverick Club for white
boys, was on hand to assist Bones. Galloway said, "Bones
already had a little organization for them—trying to give
them recreation. . . . I merely helped him put his own idea
over." The Maverick Club sponsored the Dogie Club, and
when Bones was asked about that, he answered in his trademark humorous way, "What's a maverick without a dogie?"[43]

Testimonials

Bones sort of broke a tradition in creating the Dogie Club,
for the community had always taken care of the children.
Everything had been designed for whites, and all of the
organizations and social programs were for their benefit,
while the underprivileged black children were provided for
by the black community as best as it could. But Bones wanted
the same things for his people's children, because he saw that
there were too many boys without fathers in the homes and
that they were in need of mentors—role models. Therefore,

the Dogie Club was created, and the organization would influence the lives of many youths over the years. The club did the community a great service in that it gave a lot of boys things to do, keeping them out of a lot of trouble and leading them to successful lives. Two of those youths, now senior citizens, are Charles Warford of the Walker-Warford Mortuary and Charles Kemp, a past president of the Black Cultural Center.

Activities of the Dogie Club included picnics, barbecues, camping, horse riding, and baseball. Members also took part in civic responsibilities such as improving and beautifying the community, and during the holidays, Bones and the Dogies staged Christmas-tree parties at Pioneer Hall, with all youths invited to attend for fun and games. Mike Vernon Thomas, who had been a Dogie, said, "We needed something to do and Bones gave us this club so we had something to keep us off the streets." But of course, it was more than that. Black children weren't permitted in the Maverick Club because of discrimination and segregation, and Bones demanded that they have a place to go that was similar to the Maverick Club. That was why he went to Emmett Galloway in the first place.[44]

Bones considered the Dogie Club his most important and most personal achievement, even greater than the North Heights. He had been known in the past as the greatest bronc rider on the Plains and had access to all of the public places where most blacks were denied. But those things meant little to him in those days. The Dogie Club made him swell with pride. He would invest his time and all of his money to see it through, if necessary.

Eddie Moore, another former Dogie, commented on the importance of the Dogie Club. He said, "If it hadn't been for the Dogie Club, a lot of us would have gone astray."[45]

In running the club, Bones was much more than a mentor and role model. Charles Warford clearly recalled:

Hooks would tell us why discrimination and why whites didn't want us, why we couldn't have new football suits like the white kids had. He said it was just hatred. He explained that it was prejudice and that some day it would all be over.[46]

Bones had faith in the future, although he would not live long enough to see what he envisioned. Warford probably understood Bones as well as anyone and he pointed out the activist in him that whites never realized. Bones never participated in a public march against inequality, but he spoke out in his way, quietly rather than loudly, by teaching black youngsters the true meaning of prejudice. He talked openly with them and foretold the day when the wall of hatred of one's color would be torn down and black kids would be swimming in the white pools. Bones' religious background additionally played an important role in the Dogie Club. Lonzo Aulridge, yet another former Dogie, said of Bones:

> He was peaceful. He knew the Bible pretty good, too. He quoted a lot of Scripture to us.

Aulridge said Bones also spoke of the future to them:

> "One day it will be better." He told us it wasn't going to happen overnight. He said it's going to take time. I used to ask him, Mr. Hooks, what time is it going to be [when segregation ends]? I wanted to go to the swimming pool.

But regardless of the times, Bones still tried to work with the whites. For instance, his white friend from the Maverick Club, Emmett Galloway, conducted religious services for the boys every Sunday at the three boys' clubs in Amarillo: the Maverick (white), the Dogie (black), and the Pinto (Mexican).[47]

Charles Kemp stated:

> Through the Dogies, boys regained some of the self-esteem that segregation had trampled. Bones made you feel like somebody. And to make black kids feel like they were somebody at the time was important. It was the best thing that ever happened to me.[48]

The Dogies received old, barely useable sports equipment from the Maverick Club in the same way the black schools were given useless equipment and supplies by the white schools. Charles Warford said, "It was a slap in the face, a knock on one's self esteem." Bones understood what it all meant, and still at the age of sixty-seven he continued at a determined pace, working for a world that he believed would come. He had a good many years of public service left in him and he wasn't about to quit. He believed he was too young to retire. Warford also said:

> I came from a single parent household. He [Bones] talked to us about life and good citizenship. It just made an impact on you because you believed in the person telling you.

The community needed Bones too much for him to quit.[49]

Bones' image, however, was not just for the children. He had the same reputation with adults. He never drank nor smoked, and no ugly rumors circulated about him other than the jealous gossip that is always aimed at men in similar positions. His reputation naturally played in his favor. He was known as many things: pioneer, cowboy, bronc buster, town builder, civic and social leader, peacemaker, Western philosopher, and a man beyond reproach. He was frequently sought out on the streets by old friends, acquaintances, and newspaper reporters. There was a mighty high estimation of him as a person, but Bones lived up to it. The former Dogies indicated that these things went a long way in a young boy's mind. The boys just loved the old cowboy; he was a hero and father figure, although he had no children of his own. But he did have children—he had more than a hundred adopted sons in the Dogie Club. The boys looked up to him. There was a black man in Amarillo who was something and something famous. They had Bones Hooks to admire.

Yet there was something that Bones could not quite shake

in the adult world and among his own race as well. Some in the white and black worlds resented him. Some thought he was the "whitest black man," and others didn't like the fact that he could rub elbows with influential old white men.

As a child, Charles Warford sensed the resentment and jealousy towards Bones in his own community. He felt that it was partly because Bones was an enigma but more because of his friendship with whites and his privileges. Many years later, Warford put it in perspective: "People didn't understand his connections." Likewise, Eddie Moore added:

> They didn't try to understand. They thought he was like a kind of "Uncle Tom." But he was trying to help blacks anyway he could . . . and if blacks had went along with him, he would have got a lot more done.[50]

It must be acknowledged again that the only way Bones could help his people in the predominantly white Panhandle was through his friendships with the whites. The ratio then was about 2,700 blacks to 48,000 whites.[51] Bones let the whites use him in certain ways, and he used them right back in order to get some of the good things in life for his people. How else was he to get it?There were no political organizations in place, blacks were not voting, and they were isolated from any black center of population by hundreds of miles. The only real voice they had was Bones Hooks, and he used the tools he had—the friendships and reputation he had built over forty years and a gift for getting folks to believe in his visions and help him realize them. If Bones walked a tightrope between the races, that can't be held against him. His motives were good and decent.

A Red-Letter Year

Meanwhile, Juneteenth was celebrated in 1935 at the

Jenkins Chapel in the Heights. It was the seventieth anniversary of Emancipation. J. E. Anderson was the chairman of the general committee, and the program was devoted to ex-slaves. This was probably the last Juneteenth celebration that was not held at the park commonly known as the Bones Hooks Park. (From 1950 to 1978 it was called the North Heights Park.)

Other important events that year involved the Dogie Club and Colored Panhandle Pioneer Club. After returning from the Old Settlers' Reunion, Bones attended a meeting in August of the Amarillo Council of Social Workers and asked for funding for the Dogie Club, which had exceeded 100 boys, and a girls' club that had recently been organized.[52] He had good reasons for asking for the support. His funds had been dwindling in financing the Heights, the Colored Panhandle Pioneer Club, and the Dogie Club. He had already sold off some of his real estate. The tradition of presenting white flowers to give honor to whom honor was due was costly, and he was also generous to a fault. There were few, if any, whom Bones turned down for a handout, for which he never asked payment in return.

Later that year the Dogie Club held its "annual roundup" at the "water hole" in the North Heights. The water hole was nothing more than a big hole that filled up with rainwater. It was their swimming pool, which they called "Niagara Falls," and they always enjoyed themselves there no end. However, it was a poor excuse for a swimming pool compared to the pools in the white-only parks. But Bones boasted of the Dogie Club, "We didn't have a single boy in the juvenile courts for the past sixteen months." It was not an idle boast, either. The county superintendent, Carl G. Clifft, wrote, "Not one boy has been brought before the court of Amarillo since the organization of this club." In further praise, he added, "Space will not permit me to express the measure of this man and the work he has done and is doing.

He is building for himself an everlasting monument in the influence he has upon the lives of the boys in this community."[53]

Bones' civic and social activities also reached far outside the Panhandle. Since the 1890s, when he had presented the Davis Mountain wild flowers, the guerdon of honor, at Tommy Clayton's funeral, he had consistently honored the deceased pioneers and their living families. Now he extended the tradition outside of that circle as he honored those who contributed to a better world. He even tried to bridge the gap between peoples who were not on good terms. No wonder Rev. J. L. Langston described Bones as a true "peacemaker."

For instance, the Sons of Confederate Veterans were having a difficult time finding a suitable city in which to have a reunion. Certain areas in the South were opposed to their organization, but they found a generous and hospitable town in Amarillo. Bones graciously welcomed the organization and presented a white flower as a symbol of reconciliation. One might think that Bones was wasting his time and such a gesture would go unnoticed, but apparently he got their attention and received a somewhat surprising and cordial reply.

The personal letter came from McWhorter Milner, commander of the Georgia Division, Sons of Confederate Veterans. He wrote that he was "fortunate to receive a letter and with this letter a white flower as a token of respect to the memory of the pioneers of our land." Another letter was sent from the headquarters of the United Confederate Veterans. Winnie Booth Kernan, the assistant adjutant, wrote, "I consider that the Southern people have and always will be best friends with your race, and we will dwell in this land of ours in happiness if only we will follow the Golden Rule, 'Whatsoever ye would that men should do unto you, do ye even unto them.'"[54]

Some undoubtedly questioned Bones' intentions and goodwill, for there was a growing animosity between blacks and whites, and the hostility between Northerners and Southerners was still strong, even seventy years after the Civil War's end. Furthermore, Bones had little understanding of the people from the Deep South and their motivations. Certainly, they were not the usual subjects of honor for Bones' longstanding tradition. Perhaps he believed that forgiveness and peace be offered to all people and in any situation. The man truly was a peacemaker for his times.

As 1935 came to a close, Bones turned sixty-eight. For many that is the age to slow down, smell the roses, and enjoy the rest of life. Not so for Bones—he still had much work to do. He would serve his community and country until he was no longer physically or mentally able.

CHAPTER 7

The Last Negro Cowboy
of the Plains

It is one of the traditions of the Plains to give honor to
whom honor is due.

—Bones Hooks

The depression was for real by the mid-1930s and everyone felt its effect. Many in the rural areas were forced to
come to the larger towns to look for work, and in these situations blacks were the "last hired and first fired" in order to
make room for job-seeking whites. For example, a black railroad worker entered the decade making more than two
hundred dollars a month as a porter and with double duties
as a Pullman. But when the hard times hit, the Pullman job
went to whites and the black man lost the extra income.[1]

There were other difficulties, naturally, that were not
directly related to economics but still had an impact on
Panhandle families. Beginning in 1933 and continuing for
more than a year, scores of huge black dusters devastated
the Amarillo area. April 14, 1935, was accurately labeled
"Black Easter." These dusters were largely blamed for ruin-
ing many farmers, but the worst had already come. That
occurred on January 17-18, 1934, when dust clouds rose
"10,000 feet high and rolled in from the southwest on a gale

ranging from twenty-six to sixty-one miles per hour." Sand blew for twenty-seven hours, and when the storm struck, visibility was no more than fifty feet. During each duster, houses were filled up with sand by morning, and at night people had to sleep with wet cloths over their faces so that they could breathe. Life was miserable for everyone on the Panhandle-Plains.[2]

As the mighty dusters subsided, leaders other than Bones Hooks started to emerge in the community. There were also numerous organizations by 1936 and they contributed significantly to the good of Amarillo. For example, the Negro Open Forum made a contribution to the Goodfellows, Inc., to help feed all hungry schoolchildren.[3] This points to the participation of blacks in social causes and the unity of Amarilloans during the depression. Dr. M. P. Hines, the president of the Forum, would later be prominent in several important organizations as well as civil-rights work. Also active in the community were the Eastern Star Lodge, Mt. Zion Missionary Baptist Church, the Delecta Dames Society, the Alpha Kappa Omega Club, and the Masons of the Markwell Lodge No. 415.

Another activity was a meeting arranged by J. E. Anderson of the Jenkins Chapel concerning an attack on a white police officer by three blacks. The meeting was organized to advance good citizenship. In a show of good faith, the police officers were also invited. The residents of the Heights proposed that certain citizens of good standing be deputized to patrol the Heights, as there were no black police officers and the police rarely entered the Heights. The city turned down their offer. Other activities revealed the involvement of blacks in the community, as many participated in the American Red Cross, and a number of benefits were put together to raise funds for various causes. Still, Bones remained the strongest voice in the community for the time being. He led a delegation to a City Commissioners meeting and requested that Hughes Street in the Heights be improved. He also asked for additional improvements to the park in the North Heights, and he was partially successful.[4]

Bones' activities continued to take him out of the community and even more so when they concerned Panhandle black history. The State Centennial opened in Dallas on June 6, 1936, and Bones was on hand to represent his race in the Negro Panhandle Exhibit. He brought a collection of historical items that included photographs, letters, objects, and especially his own memory of those days. He followed up the Centennial with the Juneteenth celebration at the North Heights park (it had not yet an official name) on August 27-30. The Juneteenth events focused on the celebrated anniversary of the North Heights Addition at Jenkins Chapel. Activities began with a pioneer program on Thursday night, followed by an open forum on Friday and a parade on Saturday afternoon.[5]

Bones and Dr. Wyatt

Two weeks prior to this, Bones had attended an XIT cowhands meeting, and in the first week of September he was at a Panhandle Cowboy Reunion. This was followed by an XIT Association Reunion in October. Bones was an honorary member, although the XIT was one ranch where he was never employed. In the midst of all of this, Bones found the time to take care of an important matter closer to home. He visited San Angelo to arrange for another physician to join the Amarillo community. Bones would not realize how important this recruitment would be until a few years later.

The reason for the trip was that old Dr. Ramsey was the only doctor in the community, and as numbers continued to grow he was unable to meet all of their needs. The other physician, Dr. Eugene Gravelly, had departed the Amarillo

Texas Panhandle Pioneers reunion, circa 1937. *Courtesy of the* Amarillo Globe-News.

scene. The only other doctor besides Ramsey was not a real medical doctor but an herbalist.

Somehow, Bones was introduced to Dr. J. O. Wyatt, or he was told about the man. In either case, Bones visited Dr. Wyatt and his wife, Lavernia, in San Angelo and made his proposal on behalf of Amarillo. Bones appealed to Wyatt's sense of responsibility and made a strong effort to sell the physician on the Panhandle, much in the way he sold Rev. J. L. Langston on it several years earlier. Bones appears to have been successful, for Dr. Wyatt visited Amarillo with Bones playing host, showing the physician around and introducing him to friends and citizens. After the Wyatts returned to San Angelo, they wrote a cordial letter to Bones, sincerely praising the hospitality of their host and the Amarilloans. They were particularly impressed by Lula Pierson, one of the community's esteemed ladies and pioneers in church work. She was one of the original organizers of the Mt. Zion Missionary Baptist Church and has been credited for its name. She was also influential in Langston's Church of God in Christ, which was her true denomination. Wyatt expressed a desire to move to Amarillo to set up his practice among them. He wrote, "We are hoping to come to Amarillo in the latter part of October and would like to keep in touch with you during the interim."[6] Unfortunately for Amarillo, Wyatt didn't leave San Angelo until 1937, and then he took his practice to Kerrville, where he remained for two years before finally arriving in Amarillo.

The reason for Wyatt's detour is not clear, but when he did arrive in Amarillo, he made an immediate impact with his intelligence and leadership. He approached Bones' level of leadership more than anyone else in the community, although there were others equally capable, and the two had much respect for each other.

As Christmas rolled around in 1936, Bones greeted all of Amarillo in the *Amarillo News and Globe,* but especially he greeted the old pioneers. He said, "I want to extend my best wishes to all the good people of the Panhandle, particularly the old-timers and pioneers who made this country and whose ranks are so rapidly diminishing. . . . A Merry Christmas to all the good white faces from the first old black Polled Angus that ever strayed into the herd."[7]

Meanwhile, the depression continued, and many of the lots in the North Heights owned by McSwain remained unsold and undeveloped. McSwain still tried to sell his property, but he no longer lived at Twelfth Avenue and Hughes. Times had hit him hard and he and his wife, Edith, had separated. He moved out of the house, but his wife and two sons remained there.

During this time, McSwain employed Clifford Austin as a real-estate agent to help sell lots. Austin had opened a funeral business in the Flats, the only one owned and operated by blacks. The Austin Funeral Home was located in the basement of the old Mayflower Hotel on West Second Avenue. Out of his funeral-business office, Austin sold North Heights lots to his people, and he would later relocate his own business and home there.

Clifford Austin was a unique and well-known individual. He had come from Waco, Texas, in 1929, walking the entire distance to Amarillo. When he left Waco, he had just sixteen dollars in his pocket, and by the time he arrived he still had fifteen. Austin was a bright young man and quickly found work with one of Amarillo's successful families, the Allen Early family. In Early's employ he was chauffeur, cook, gardener, babysitter, and anything else that was required. Allen Early, Jr., liked to say, "It looked like we had a lot of servants because Clifford did everything."[8]

Austin had made an acquaintance with Bones soon after settling in town and they became fast and lasting friends. Bones and another leader, dentist Dr. M. P. Hines, took him under their wings and encouraged him to attend mortuary school, a profession that their community much needed.

Austin took their advice and graduated from the School of Mortuary Science at Fort Worth, Texas, in 1934. This was one of the few integrated fields, and Austin graduated with the son of the popular funeral director E. M. Blackburn. There was not a great demand for Austin's services right away, as the local black population was fairly young, but he was prepared. The blacks who did pass away were handled by white funeral-home directors such as Blackburn and N. S. Griggs. Thus, Austin continued to work for the Early family, but he told Allen Early, Sr., that he desired to go into the mortuary business.

Within a few years and with Early's help, Austin opened up his own funeral business. This was 1937, and that's when Clifford Austin's brother, Cleve (Cleveland), arrived in Amarillo. Cleve was soon introduced to Bones and they became great friends. In fact, Cleve may have had a closer relationship to Bones than Clifford had. He was the old cowboy's personal chauffeur whenever Bones presented the lone white flower at a home or meeting. Cleve also accompanied Bones on at least one important interview, because Bones never learned to drive.

Cleve Austin had intended only to visit Amarillo. In Waco, he had worked at a private golf course, often competing with—and beating—the resident pro. The pro, realizing Cleve's potential, told him to go north or east, where he might be able to make a living at golf. Cleve never got out of Amarillo, but years later, after the end of segregation, Cleve won several tournaments around the country, including tournaments in San Francisco, New Orleans, Las Vegas, and Atlanta.[9] If not for the times, when racism prevailed, he might have accomplished feats similar to those of Tiger Woods.

The same year Cleve came to Amarillo to help his brother in the funeral business, Edith McSwain and her two sons were having a very hard time and looking for a way to get out of debt. They sold their home for almost five thousand dollars cash to Clarence Watley. That was a considerable sum during the depression, and the money paid off Mrs. McSwain's debts. They moved into town, and the house was thereafter known as the "Watley Mansion."[10]

Jennie Watley raised two sons, Clarence and Elbert, without the help of a husband and supported her family by operating the Watley Hotel out of her home in the Flats, where she built up a considerable business. She eventually deeded the hotel to Clarence, who was becoming an entrepreneur in his own right. Clarence Watley had interests in several other businesses, one being the Working Men's Social Club and Parlor, which was simply a pool hall and smoking room where the young men hung out and kept off the streets. He operated that business from the 1930s to about 1956. The Watleys were one of the wealthiest black families in Amarillo due to their numerous businesses and real-estate holdings, and the Watley Subdivision was established in Miller Heights near the Mathew Hooks Subdivision.[11]

Bones and the First Lady

Meanwhile, Bones took trips over much of the country—that is, wherever the Santa Fe line went, because he had a lifetime pass on the Santa Fe Railroad. He visited Chicago, St. Louis, Kansas City, Detroit, and other locations to present black history. These journeys no doubt educated him on the conditions in some of the bigger cities, yet the highlight for him occurred not in any of these places but back in Amarillo. The First Lady, Eleanor Roosevelt, arrived in town in March 1938, just in time for the Mother-in-Law Parade on March 9, a celebration unique to Amarillo. It was started by Gene Howe, then publisher of the *Amarillo News and Globe*, who organized it after offending his own mother-in-law. Bones presented the First Lady with a lone white flower, the guerdon of honor, which was overshadowed by a "bouquet of over 5,000 roses," weighing about 2,500 pounds, that the city of Amarillo presented to her. It is not known whether Amarillo received a warm and personal note from her for such a grand gesture, but Bones did. The First Lady thanked him for the flower and the honor and added, "How glad I was to meet you." She also mentioned his "granddaughter" and hoped the little girl had a wonderful life. Of course, this was not Bones' granddaughter but more likely one of the girls from the girls' club, probably Gloria Fay Foster.[12]

Pres. Franklin D. Roosevelt followed the First Lady to Amarillo in hot July that same year. It was a huge event that was interrupted by rain at Ellwood Park. Bones was on hand as usual but did not present the president with a lone white flower. He had already given him that honor five years earlier through U.S. Congressman Marvin Jones. Bones received a reply from the president as well, but it was from the White House staff on governmental stationery and not nearly as personal as the First Lady's letter.[13]

Bones turned seventy-one in November and he still had a

Bones Hooks on Polk Street, circa 1940. *Courtesy of the* Amarillo
Globe-News.

spry jump in his step. He was often seen on Polk Street and he kept up his memberships in some of the old organizations. Reporters were still interviewing him about the old days and it seemed that someone might write a book on his life and experiences, but it never happened.

Then Dr. J. O. Wyatt finally moved his practice and family to Amarillo. Within just a few years, he would be a prominent citizen of the town and a major property holder in the North Heights and Miller Heights. For now, though, it was slow going, as he was the new doctor in town and most preferred the old trusted physician, Dr. Ramsey.

Bones was traveling again in 1939. This time he journeyed to Detroit to represent his race in the "Seventy-Five Years of Negro Progress" exhibit. Wherever Bones went, he definitely stood out from the rest of the crowd. For instance, when he wore his boots, riding pants, and Stetson in Kansas City, people knew right away that he was from the West. He went to Chicago and it was the same. So when he went to Detroit, he vowed it would be different this time. He recalled:

> I put my boots and Stetson in a sack and shipped them home. I went to a store and bought me a blue suit and a little hat. But they still said, "He's from Texas." If it ain't the way you look, it's the way you talk and act. No matter what a Texan does or says, when he gets through he's still a Texan.[14]

If the 1930s seem to have been Bones' decade, that is because it was. He dominated the Amarillo scene with his charisma and accomplishments. Although the racial lines were hard and strict, Bones doesn't seem to have noticed them much regarding himself. Instead, he was concerned about his people, and he understood that when all of his old pioneer friends were gone, so would be his position among the whites. That may be why he never stopped working for the black community.

Bones Pays His Respects

Then a tragic accident occurred in the white world that affected Bones. Julian and Billy Bivins, the son and grandson of Lee Bivins, were killed while hunting coyotes from their airplane over North Amarillo on Bivins' property. With heartfelt sadness, Bones presented the Bivins family with two white flowers, one each for the deceased, and he respectfully mentioned the memory of Lee Bivins. Shortly thereafter, he received a letter from Miles Bivins, thanking him for the tribute and stating that the "mention of my father was particularly appreciated."[15]

Cleve Austin, Bones' good friend, couldn't help but remember that day and the solemn occasion, as he was Bones' chauffeur. Bones and Cleve did not approach the rear entrance, as blacks were expected to do. Bones wasn't accustomed to doing so and didn't do it now. He went to the front door and knocked. The Bivinses received them into the house. Bones had given Cleve one white carnation and kept the other. Bones put his flower on Julian's coffin and Cleve placed his on Billy's. Cleve knew that if he hadn't been with Bones, he would have had to go to the rear, but not on this day—not with Bones Hooks. The old cowboy had that much respect from the pioneer families, even so long after Lee Bivins' death.[16]

By this time, Bones had used up much of his financial resources, yet he kept the Dogie Club going and he never turned down a kid who wanted to join. However, Pioneer Hall was in deep financial trouble and had been neglected. It was now mortgaged to various persons, some of whom were friends, and there seemed to be no reasonable way to pay it off. Neither was it the social and civic center it used to be. Bones no longer lived at Pioneer Hall nor the Heights; he had a new official address in the Flats. Other people ran Pioneer Hall, and they exercised little authority and control. The weekend dances that had originally been held to offset costs had now turned rough. Some were referring to Pioneer Hall as "Murderer's Hall" and not without good reason. It was now not much more than a nightclub. Being a man who never smoked nor drank, Bones must have objected to the way of life at Pioneer Hall. The Dogie Club didn't meet there anymore; they met at the park in the North Heights or someplace else. Bones often took them to a place northwest of the Heights out near the old smelter, where they camped out and barbecued.[17]

Bones Sells Pioneer Hall

Then a ray of hope shone out of nowhere, an almost divine solution that would bring Pioneer Hall out of its recent darkness and return to it a high purpose. That hope came in the form of Rev. James J. Regan, O.P. Father Regan wanted to purchase Pioneer Hall and turn it into a Catholic mission. He had come to Amarillo on October 15, 1940, and was assigned to start a mission among blacks, the first ever in the Texas Panhandle. He started his mission on the busy and sometimes volatile West Third Avenue in the Flats. Originally called "Our Lady of the Rosary Mission," it was no more than one small room with thin walls. His Mass was often interrupted by rude and violent noises outside the walls.[18]

Just the same, Regan made quick inroads into the neighborhood and his small mission was well received, soon becoming overcrowded with converts. He saw that a much larger place was needed for his vision, and he learned that Bones Hooks, the old cowboy, might be willing to sell Pioneer Hall. The two-story building in the Heights was just what Regan had been praying for. Finally, in July of 1941, a deal was made for the sum of $5,000, much less than the building had originally cost, but there were problems. Bones was no longer the sole owner of the building. Other names now appeared on the deed, including J. O. Wyatt and M. P. Hines. Furthermore, Regan had no money. The transaction was based on faith and promises made between the two parties. Ownership was transferred, and the local leaders and Bones were pleased and relieved that Pioneer Hall would cease to exist as a nightclub and once again make a real contribution to the community.[19]

So Pioneer Hall passed into history and became the Blessed Saint Martin de Porres Mission, named after a dark-skinned Peruvian saint, probably of African descent. Before long, there was a chapel for the worshipers and a clinic for the poor and terminally ill. In a way, Bones' first vision of the building being a hospital for his people had come true. It was certainly the only clinic of its kind in the Panhandle, although it was more of a care facility for blacks than a hospital. Shortly afterwards, the Dominican Sisters from Columbus, Ohio, arrived to start a parish school, which would serve the community well in the hard times to come.[20]

Wartime

In the same year that the mission was dedicated, the U.S. entered World War II after Pearl Harbor was attacked on December 7, 1941. The war devastated everyone and brought America together for the time being, putting racial differences on the back burner. It would also provide Bones with a patriotic project. Bones and Clifford Austin both served the war effort on the home front as agents for the Advisory Board for Registrants, and they received commendations from the Selective Service for their efforts in enlisting area blacks into military service.[21]

One of the Dogies to join the marines was Paul Eugene Shorten, who had been the president of the Dogie Club for three terms. He was the son of Phillip and Lanoria Shorten,

Dogie Club, 1940s. *Courtesy of the* Amarillo Globe-News.

early leaders in Amarillo. Phillip came to Amarillo about 1907 and had privileges similar to Bones', only not so extensive. He was friends with H. P. Canode and W. H. Fuqua, had access to banks and white physicians, and may have been the first black to own property in the Flats. He and Lanoria were original members of the Mt. Zion Missionary Baptist Church when it was officially established in 1916. Lanoria came from an impressive background, as her mother, Texana, was a missionary of renown. But Lanoria made an even stronger impact in just a few short years. Her exceptional voice was in demand all over the Panhandle and she was known as the "Nightingale of the West." Lanoria, Bob Handy, and Genoa Dixon all had spots on a local radio station that is now known as KGNC. Paul was also involved at the station, acting as a disc jockey before racial problems forced him to leave. He was undoubtedly the first black radio disc jockey in Amarillo.[22]

Bones had never been in the military. He was almost fifty years old when World War I began, and as the U.S. entered World War II, he was seventy-four. But that did not prevent him from getting involved and encouraging a number of former Dogies to enlist. Although he received a medal for his work, he knew that those truly deserving medals and commendations were the young black men who went off to war in Europe and the Pacific, sacrificing their lives for world freedom while being denied the same freedom at home.

One of those courageous young men who was lucky enough to return home alive and in one piece was Charles Warford, a former Dogie whose education had been cut short by the draft. He entered the navy, and during his tour of duty he had no permanent base, as he was always at sea. He crossed the Atlantic Ocean twelve times, where he saw action against the German submariners, and in the Pacific he saw battle with the Japanese Kamikaze pilots. Warford, like so many others, was never awarded any medal or commendation for such extensive and hazardous duty, but perhaps he should have.

While in these situations, Warford learned some of the things that Bones had learned on the frontier in the pioneer days—that people often had to rely on one another for survival regardless of personal beliefs and prejudices. For instance, when they were under attack from the enemy, there was little thought of the racism that had been evident beforehand. As was mentioned in chapter 3, Warford especially noticed that some West Virginia "rednecks" on his ship abandoned their bigotry when all the men aboard united to fight the same enemy. But when they all got back to the States, as Warford remembered, some of the boys went back to their old ways.[23]

Back home, some blacks did not serve in the military when drafted. Some may have refused or could not be found, but others, such as Clifford and Cleve Austin, were exempt because of their profession. Both brothers tried to register but were denied. They were the only blacks in Amarillo in the funeral business, and they were going to be needed at home, as some of their own were going to return in a box. There was no shame in their exemption, for they served their country as their government requested.

Being a healthy man and in uniform, Cleve Austin was subjected to some mistreatment, or rather, racism at the hands of an unpopular Texas Ranger. One day Cleve was at the Harlem Grill, owned by Gabe Carthen and a busy hangout in the Flats. A Texas Ranger walked in and saw Cleve in his everyday street clothes. The Ranger immediately accosted him, asking Cleve if he had a draft card. Cleve told the Ranger that he did and added, "Want me to get it out?" The Ranger didn't even want to see it. He didn't care if Cleve had one or not. He slapped Cleve across the face—to the protests of Gabe Carthen—and hauled him off to jail. At the jail, the sheriff wanted to know what Cleve Austin was being arrested for, as he was known by the sheriff and many other prominent whites in Amarillo. "Draft dodger," the Ranger answered. Cleve remained in jail until word got around to Charlie Fisk, president of the First National Bank, who immediately got him out. Fisk was angry that Cleve had been arrested for no good reason and made a promise to him: "He [the Ranger] won't be here long." And he wasn't. Fisk kept his word and, using his connections, had the Ranger run out of town.[24]

Such things never happened to Bones. Usually, the local authorities dealt with *him* in regard to the black community. The U.S. government did the same—and quite frequently during the war. There were much younger men, such as Clifford Austin, who had lots of energy, but it was probably through Congressman Marvin Jones that Bones was highly recommended for other government service.

During the fall of 1942, the Defense Recreational Council was addressing recreational problems for soldiers and defense workers, and Colonel Simpson at the Amarillo Air Base requested Bones' input in regard to black airmen. Bones had the opportunity to voice his opinions at a dinner Simpson held at the Amarillo Hotel.[25] He considered it an honor to participate, but it also pointed to the segregation in the military.

Bones also used his participation in the military to present the guerdon of honor to those deserving. Early in 1943 he honored a young woman, Myrtle Volgamore of Portales,

Old-timers' reunion, 1941. Left to right: Lonnie Jones, Bones Hooks, Rich Crump, Gene Ellison, and Hawley Plemons. *Courtesy of the* Amarillo Globe-News.

Pioneer reunion, 1943, probably near Canyon, Texas. Bones Hooks is standing second from left. *Courtesy of the* Amarillo Globe-News.

New Mexico. Bones had always greatly respected the women pioneers and Miss Volgamore was a true pioneer in her own right. According to Bones' information, she was one of the first women to become a member of the Bluebonnet Squadron of the U.S. Navy Women's Reserve. He sent a letter with the flower in honoring her. He wrote, "I wish to pay a tribute of respect to you with a lone white flower, a guerdon of honor, that one of our group has been sending for the past forty-eight years in honor of the pioneer men and women who have helped build this great empire of ours here on the Plains. For it is women of your type and organizations of this kind that can make a Democracy live, and it is one of the traditions of the Plains to give honor to whom honor is due." The letter additionally revealed Bones' position in the community by the way it was signed: "Committee of Churches of the Colored Citizens of Amarillo, Texas, Mathew Bones Hooks."[26]

The U.S. Civil Service Calls

The Tenth United States Civil Service called on Bones by letter in 1943 at his residence and Dogie Club business address, 304 West Second Avenue. The office that contacted him wanted his assistance in recruiting "qualified personnel for various jobs from among the Colored population of the Panhandle-Plains." More specifically, they were seeking young black women who could type and do stenography and would relocate to Washington, D.C. The letter originated in New Orleans, Louisiana, and a representative, James H. Clark, later came to Amarillo and paid Bones a formal visit. His journey was not in vain, as Bones was willing and able to help in any way that he could. He was only seventy-five years old.[27]

Bones was also heavily involved with black troops at the

Amarillo Air Base by summer and he persuaded his pioneer friends to assist. They planned to entertain airmen in cooperation with the base and the USO. The event was to be a "Traditional Badger Night at the USO auditorium that would portray early pioneer traditions [and] give the boys a touch of the real West." Bones initiated this program, with the cooperation of the "Colored" USO in the Flats, as his letter to the "Officer In Charge of Negro Troops" indicates. Not only did they entertain the airmen with history of the Panhandle in the pioneer days, but they educated those who knew little, if anything at all, about the subject, which was very important to Bones. He wanted these young black men to return home one with knowledge of Panhandle history, particularly the history of black cowboys. He gave them a history that had nothing to do with the cheap novels and movies that depicted an all-white West without the real contributions of blacks. As blacks were being excluded from history lessons, Bones was doing his share to tell how the West was really won. Also notable at this time was the way Bones had started signing his name: "Bones Hooks, Negro Pioneer Cowhand." This pointed to his preoccupation with the pioneers and the old cowboy traditions of the Plains.[28]

Meanwhile, the deep-rooted cowboy tradition of the white flower kept going. It had reached far outside of Texas, even to Europe, to dignitaries such as the prime minister of England, Winston Churchill. But one touching and tragic response to a presentation of the guerdon of honor particularly meant a great deal to him, perhaps more than the acknowledgment from world leaders such as Churchill and Roosevelt. Early in August 1942, Bones had presented Lt. Paul Ross Barnard, U.S.M.A.C., with a lone white flower at the Sky Buster Battalion banquet in the Crystal Ballroom of Amarillo's Herring Hotel. A year later, almost to the day, Barnard's plane went down in the line of duty off the coast of Florida and he perished. The flower that Bones had presented to him was discovered neatly pressed in his Bible, revealing its significance to the lieutenant. Bones received a moving letter from Barnard's brother, Pvt. O. C. Barnard, who thought he would like to know how Paul went down and what the flower had meant to him.[29] Bones deeply appreciated it.

Bones participated in the Old Settlers' Reunion in the middle of September and was reminded that there weren't going to be many more, as the numbers of the old pioneers were quickly dwindling. He told a reporter:

> I've seen most of the old cowmen pass on. . . . I have a list of these pioneers that are left, but it's growing small. I haven't counted up to see how many there are left on that list 'cause I know it's getting up close to my name.[30]

Bones Sits on the Grand Jury

Towards the end of the war, Bones seemed more and more preoccupied with the white-flower tradition and the passing on of the last pioneers. Indeed the war effort and the pioneers took up much of his time, and he spread himself thin trying to do too much. Yet he received a personal honor that broke down one more racial barrier. He was selected in April 1945 to sit on the Potter County grand jury. He was the first black ever to sit on a grand jury in the entire Panhandle. As was his custom, he presented the grand jury with the guerdon of honor. He also shared the session with a fellow cowboy and pioneer, John Arnot, who had been in the Panhandle about as long as Bones.[31]

Taking his place on the jury meant a lot to Bones and he deemed it not only an honor but a privilege. Justice was in the jury's hands and he believed in the democratic system, even as his people were denied the right to vote as well as many other rights. He viewed the jury similar to vigilantes or a mob in that he believed that no matter how mean and ugly it might get, there was always one good person willing to stand up for the truth. He never lost faith in what he had always told the boys in the Dogie Club: "Someday it would all be over." He prayed that he'd see the day when it would be common for blacks to sit on the grand jury.

Bones had bestowed the guerdon of honor upon a number of white individuals and pioneer families, and it might appear that he had neglected to honor his own people, but that was not the case. When Joe Louis arrived in Amarillo in 1944 to put on a boxing exhibition for the soldiers at the air base, Bones presented the great fighter with the traditional white flower. Jackie Robinson, the baseball pioneer, was also presented the guerdon of honor. Much closer to home, Bones honored Frank and Myrtle Martin on their twenty-fifth wedding anniversary.[32] Frank first came to Amarillo about 1909-10, when the Christians were having religious services in servant quarters. He was an original member and trustee of the Mt. Zion Missionary Baptist Church and a community leader. He operated the Martin Hotel, and *The Progress Magazine* was published out of one of its rooms, as he worked hard to improve race relations in Amarillo. He was certainly a worthy honoree and only one of the community who was so honored by Bones.

Last Cowboy Reunion

The war had finally ended and Bones' work among the airmen also concluded. He celebrated his seventy-eighth birthday and still felt unfulfilled. He had yet to see his vision of equality come to pass, and there was some unfinished business with the the pioneers who were heading down their last trail. Bones wanted a true honor bestowed upon the pioneer women of the Panhandle-Plains. It should have been done a long time ago by the men pioneers, but it wasn't. Now there weren't many of these men left, and time was running out. There were so few that 1946 would be the last roundup of the Western Cowpunchers Association. Bones pleaded with his group to do the right thing and make "a lasting memorial to the women pioneers." He wrote a unique and emotional letter to Mel Armstrong, president of the association, that contained some of Bones' most eloquent words.

> For those mothers came from good homes to this country in the early days and lived in dugouts and worked and fought by the side of their men that their children might enjoy the great things we have here today. Long ago, cowboys, pioneers and nesters would go to Canyon in wagons, buckboards, horseback, any way they could get there and stay for ten days of friendship. They'd make a city out of wagons and tents, cook, eat and sleep on the ground. At night they would sit around the campfires and tell of the good things that would come to the Plains. Today on the same spot is the State Teachers College and their sons, daughters, grandsons and granddaughters are going to school there. . . . In man's day, we built Tascosa and Boot Hill; when women came, churches, schools, home comforts, all the good things of life began to be brought in. Why not build a monument to their efforts and accomplishments?
>
> For their efforts were tireless and their course undaunted. You men are living witnesses to the part they played in helping build what we now have here. . . . Now cowboys, let's do this one more thing! Where the last stand of the cowboys will be, Let's build a monument to the Pioneer Mothers of the Panhandle Country for it is one of the traditions of the cowboy to give honor to whom honor is due. Why not build this memorial to these women on the last roundup ground? This Panhandle is being peopled by new people today and there are not many pioneers left. Let the new people know what the cowboy was like. This flower is presented to the President and the members of

the Western Cowpunchers Association who will give it to the oldest man present. He in turn will give it to the oldest woman present—thus, it reaches the Real pioneer builders of our civilization.

Mathew Bones Hooks,
the Last Living Negro Cowboy of the Plains[33]

Bones' efforts were not rewarded, and in fact, to this day a monument to the pioneer women has not been dedicated. Perhaps there were just too few pioneers around to do the job. More likely, it was still a man's world and women didn't have many more rights than blacks. Whatever the case, it was one of Bones' few goals that was within sight but not reached. Age and frailty were already against him, and this would be his last big project.

Bones remained a cowboy throughout his entire life, but after that year there would be no more reunions. For the past few years he had seen himself as the caretaker of the pioneers, and before long, the last living pioneers would be standing by him instead.

CHAPTER 8

Down the Last Trail

In the old days, no one asked a man his name or where he was from. He was just accepted as a man, a friend.

—Bones Hooks

O! Beat the drum slowly
And play the fife lowly—
Play the death march as you carry me along.
Take me to the green valley—
Then lay the sod o'er me
For I'm an old cowboy.
—Jerry Mailin, *Amarillo Globe-News,* February 6, 1951

Few people have had a day established in their name while they were still alive. Bones Hooks Day was an honor that his people bestowed upon Bones for all of the things he had accomplished and even his honorable efforts that had failed. It was started about 1941 by the Amarillo Negro Business League, on the fifty-fourth anniversary of Bones' white-flower tradition. May 5 was set aside as the day of honor.

By 1947 Bones had stepped aside and passed the mantle of leadership to others, but he remained a spokesperson for his people. One of the new leaders to succeed Bones was Dr.

One of the last photographs of Bones Hooks, circa 1947. *Courtesy of the* Amarillo Globe-News.

J. O. Wyatt. After less than a decade in Amarillo, he had proven himself an excellent physician and an even better businessman. Cleve Austin fondly recalled Wyatt's business style with a chuckle. Wyatt "wanted his money" from his patients, and if he didn't get a full payment for the services rendered, he reminded you about it the next time he saw you. He was just as insistent when it came to business outside of his practice. He heavily invested in real-estate ventures in the North Heights and Miller Heights. In July 1945, he purchased some foreclosed property in the North Heights that consisted of forty-four lots. An earlier acquisition, and probably his most important, was ten lots in Miller Heights, bought from friends Rev. J. L. and Scelestine Langston for $450. This included an old two-story hotel or rooming house in much need of repair. The building became the Wyatt Memorial Hospital, and adjacent was a small house that would be used as nurse quarters. The deal for the property was finalized in June of 1944. According to records, a building permit was granted in 1945 and an addition was constructed in 1948. When it opened, the Wyatt Memorial Hospital had sixteen beds. Because of the times, it was the only place in Amarillo where Dr. Wyatt was permitted to practice.[1]

Wyatt was a different type of man than Bones. He had never accepted segregation and he faced it head on. He didn't have Bones' connections or charisma, but he would successfully steer his people onwards in his own way. However, his victories would also bring open hatred and threats of violence to him and his family. If he was bitter that he could not practice in the white hospitals, he was certainly justified. While blacks could be treated down in the basement of the white Northwest Hospital, he was not permitted to treat his own people. That was the purpose behind establishing the Wyatt Memorial Hospital, the first of its kind in the Panhandle. Unfortunately, it was inadequate for the most serious cases, lacking proper equipment and medicines. But it served his people until he could get the laws changed so that he could practice in the white hospitals and have access to modern equipment and supplies.

During Wyatt's rise to leadership, Bones was a friend and supporter of the doctor. Bones' main activities after the war were the continuation of the Dogie Club and looking after the old pioneers. No longer did he sign his correspondences as "The Spokesman of the Colored Race" but now exclusively as "Mathew Bones Hooks, the Last Living Negro Cowboy of the Plains." He told a reporter, "I now spend my time looking after the pioneers."[2] Nevertheless, he was not entirely finished with public service. He was often the speaker or guest of honor at banquets organized to raise money for various causes. As he was honored time and time again at these functions, the Dogie Club carried on. However, the Lobo Club and others were trying to purchase a building that might serve as a community center and youth club. Bones, of course, lent his name and body any way that he could and took a backseat to the other leaders, who now included Dr. J. O. Wyatt, Dr. M. P. Hines, Rev. Robert Hines, W. G. Crawford, Rev. J. L. Langston, and Rev. R. N. Marshburn.

Bones kept up his activity as long as he could. Then in 1949, his health significantly weakened, and the following year he became seriously ill. The illness would be prolonged and he would never recover. He went to live with his brother for awhile but, dissatisfied, he returned to Amarillo. Up until this illness overtook Bones, except for his injury while employed on the Santa Fe he had never been very sick nor even under a doctor's care.

His finances were exhausted by this time and he lived at the Gray Hotel on his meager railroad pension. Over the years he had never turned anyone down for a loan or handout, and some had taken advantage. Those people believed that he always had plenty and that the white folks just gave him things, but that was a misconception. He paid for every piece of land, building, and personal possession, not to mention the expensive tradition of the white flower. He didn't take charity. He paid his own way. The white man gave him little, except for the friendship, mutual respect, and unending trust of the pioneers.

During the fifty-four years that he had presented the white flower, he had honored 293 pioneer families and 410 men and women who had passed away.[3] The list is almost endless, from world leaders to celebrities who broke racial barriers to faceless pioneers who helped change the untamable Plains. He never failed to "give honor to whom honor was due" regardless of race, religion, or sex, as Rev. J. L. Langston pointed out long ago.

When the illness became too severe and he was bedridden, Bones was taken from his room at the Gray Hotel and moved to the Wyatt Memorial Hospital. The new people of the Plains didn't know Bones and he wasn't given special care or privileges at the white hospital as he might have in times past. He remained under Wyatt's care for a time until his remaining funds ran out. What was the old bronc buster to do? Before long, Wyatt announced that Bones was well enough to leave the hospital, but medically advised, "He will need constant companionship, day and night." Bones returned to his room at the Gray Hotel, and he received many visitors who were concerned about him. Old friends such as Clifford and Cleve Austin and Rev. J. L. Langston were frequently at his bedside, but there was little they could do. He seemed to be just holding on.[4]

Friends from all over the Panhandle heard that Bones was gravely ill, and the local newspapers carried daily updates of his condition. The outpouring of love and friendship was just overwhelming. Friends, white and black, sent get-well cards and monetary donations to help him get along in his time of need. Most donations were anonymous, as Bones' cowboy pride was widely known. The *Amarillo Daily News* received so much money for him that it established a "Bones Hooks Fund," to be overseen by Grady Camp. Leecie Silas, a maid at the Amarillo Hotel, was hired from this fund to take care of Bones in her home.[5]

Declining Health

Eventually, "Old Bones" grew worse, and much of the time he hardly recognized anyone. It was difficult for old friends to see him in this condition. However, he did have some good days and when he was in a clear state of mind he remembered everything and everyone. On one of those days he remembered a debt that he owed. With just fifty dollars to his name, he insisted on using twenty-three dollars of it to pay off the debt, saying, "My word. I gave my word I'd have his money today." His word of honor still prevailed to the very end. It was this virtue that had enabled him to make so many true and lasting friends, cut across so many racial barriers, and accomplish so much in his lifetime. His word meant even more to him than his own welfare. Bones and his word of honor were inseparable. Many years before, Bones had made a statement that proved true:

> What's in a man will come out sooner or later. I've seen men start with a trail herd and plenty of pep. But after a day or two on the trail the drag man will be back with the drag cattle.[6]

Bones was never a drag man. What was inside of him had been coming out all of these years. And it still came out of him on his deathbed. What came out was pure honor.

One day in early February 1951, Bones was in his right mind again. He was in a good mood—joking, peaceful— and had been praying to God. He told Mrs. Silas:

> Of course, I know I'm going to die. But don't worry. I feel wonderful.

Bones was at peace with God and must have realized his eternal fate, and he knew it was good. He then gave Mrs. Silas a stern lecture on her tobacco habit. That same night, about 9:30, Bones peacefully died in his sleep.[7]

He was eighty-three years old and had lived seventy-three of those years in West Texas and the Panhandle. It is worth repeating that he was one of the last of the cowboys and pioneers who had lived in this region when it was nothing but prairie land. He had been a man of both legendary and real proportions. If he had been white, he would have inspired novels and movies. But Western history had overlooked him because of the color of his skin. Just like other black cowboys, pioneers, heroes, and legends, he had been written out of history.

The Funeral

Yet Bones was not forgotten. Amarillo had not overlooked him—all of its citizenry was in mourning. His death was taken hard by blacks and whites alike. More than fifty years earlier, Bones had begun practicing the cowboy tradition of honor when he presented his first white flowers to Tommy Clayton. Its meaning of giving honor to whom honor is due was part of the legendary cowboy code. By the time the last white flower was presented, more than seven hundred had been given to pioneers and dignitaries the world over. As the mourners gathered to pay their final respects to an old pioneer and friend, the tradition of the guerdon of honor was bestowed upon Bones in a most fitting manner, a touching tribute of love and honor that moved the entire city. Perhaps no Amarillo funeral had been as large as that of Lee Bivins, but no funeral had been as emotional nor broken down so many race barriers, at least for one day, as that of Mathew ("Bones") Hooks. Hundreds of white flowers, more than Bones had ever sent personally, flooded the church from all over the Panhandle, offered to him in death as a worthy and real tribute. And there was not a dry eye in the building.[8]

The services were held at a pioneer church, Mt. Zion Missionary Baptist Church, in the heart of the Flats, and Rev. R. N. Marshburn was the officiating pastor. There was not room enough for all of the visitors that day, as blacks and whites were ushered in shoulder to shoulder at full capacity in a final tribute and farewell to a beloved old friend. The races had grown significantly apart in the past decades, and their differences were clearer than ever before. Not on this day, however—there was peace and harmony, even if only temporarily.

The honorary pallbearers were the "graying pioneers from the Old Settlers' Reunion of the Tri-State" and the descendants of those already gone. Among them were Mel Armstrong, John Snyder, Judge Henry Bishop, Col. W. S. Williams, Lon Sellars, Bill Thompson, N. S. Griggs, and Joe Williams. Joe Williams was the only man still living with whom Bones had broken wild horses. This had been at the RO Ranch near Clarendon.[9]

Active pallbearers were from the Lobo Club. This was fitting, for they had previously inducted Bones into the organization as a lifetime honorary member, and it would be the Lobo Club who would put a marker on Bones' grave. The pallbearers were Dr. J. O. Wyatt, Dr. M. P. Hines, John Sanders, J. W. Wilson, R. W. ("Bob") Handy, and J. P. Hyman. Among the white guests was John Trollinger, a friend of fifty-three years, who walked down the aisle and placed a lone white flower on the coffin, in the same way that a flower had been placed on Tommy Clayton's coffin about fifty-eight years earlier. Inspiring music filled the air, and then Joe Williams, representing the Tri-State pioneers, gave Bones a worthy, personal, and sincere tribute.[10]

According to the *Amarillo Daily News*, Dr. Wyatt also paid tribute to Bones. Pastor Marshburn spoke with deep respect of Bones' accomplishments, Rev. J. S. Thomas read from Scripture, and Rev. J. W. Wade presented the prayer. The requiem was by Mrs. K. O. Hines, Vernon Hines sang "I've Done My Work," and the Senior Choir, founded by Carrie Peal Hines, performed the choral music. A long procession of automobiles then left the church for Llano Cemetery, where the dignified cowboy and leader of his people was laid to rest in his final campground, next to his first wife, Indiana Crenshaw.

Thus, it was finished. Bones had "fought the good fight . . . finished the race."

Bones' death brought an era to an end. He was one of the last of his breed. He had believed in the code of honor as a cowboy in the pioneer days, and he had lived by that same code as a leader of his people. For most of the past fifty years almost the entire load of leadership had been on his shoulders. Never again would one person carry that kind of load, nor would anyone enjoy the same kind of relationship with the whites that Bones had. The new leaders would rely more on their numbers and organization than friendship, and they would make demands, not ask for cooperation. They could not use Bones' methods, and no one had his appeal. If they had tried it his way, the new leaders would have completely failed. Bones had always done it his way and lived his life his way.

Now, things would be very different.

Conclusion

The name Bones would be recognized beyond the Panhandle long after his death, even to the present. Following the funeral, many resolved to carry on the Dogie Club and the white-flower tradition in his name. But truthfully, the Dogie Club was no longer necessary, as the Lobo Club secured and sponsored the old Patten High School as a community center. As for the white-flower tradition, it was a cowboy tradition, and there was no one else able to fulfill it as Bones had. When Bones died, so did this unique tradition on the Panhandle-Plains.

Bones' accomplishments were many, but he did not get to see his vision of equality realized in his lifetime. He never doubted that it would come and discrimination would fade away. He consistently told the Dogies that someday everything would be different, but those kinds of changes came only after his death.

Some changes came shortly after he was laid to rest, due to his years of unselfishly preparing the groundwork that would make them occur much easier in the Panhandle than in other parts of the country. Discrimination was first cracked in the area of education, and it occurred well before Rosa Parks' great sit-down on that bus in Alabama.

Bones' work brought this about, without a single shot or violent confrontation.

This particular project began in February 1948. The Amarillo College Board approved a proposal by the town's emerging leaders that "authorized night classes for graduates of Carver High." (Carver High had replaced the old Patten High.) The "Negro Day Nursery" was considered as a site, but it was quite inadequate and never came to pass. By March of 1949 the college board offered only "vocational classes at Carver High School for Negro residents." Community leaders and members of the Carver High PTA rejected the board's proposal. A delegation that included Dr. J. O. Wyatt, Rev. R. H. Hines, Dr. M. P. Hines, Rev. J. L. Langston, and Thomas J. White met with the board and argued that "Negro citizens were tax payers supporting Amarillo College" and that "there were laws requiring equal facilities for blacks." The board gave in a little, and the result was junior-college courses and facilities at Carver High, to begin September 1, 1951.[1]

In May 1951, the board members met at Carver High with those whom they considered prospective college students. Unknown to them, there had been much unrest in the community regarding college classes and integration, and new demands were presented—not by the students but the Council of Community Organizations, leading citizens, and members of the Carver PTA. The president of the council was W. G. Crawford, and other members were Rev. R. H. Hines and Dr. J. O. Wyatt. Pastor Hines asked several questions of the board. He wanted to know how the college would be administered, who would teach the courses, what courses would be available, and so on. Dr. Wyatt, however, openly addressed the issue of segregation and informed the board that classes at Carver were unacceptable. Members of the council and PTA backed him up in this stance.[2] The board members were outmaneuvered, but it was not over yet.

After a discussion, the board refused to approve their demands and still planned to have junior-college courses at Carver under segregated circumstances. Then another delegation appeared before the board in October; they were W. G. Crawford, Rev. R. N. Marshburn, David Hughes, and Dr. J. O. Wyatt. They cited discrimination in the Amarillo College practices and proposed rather strongly that their children be admitted to the college. A long discussion followed and the board promptly voted. The decision might have surprised the delegation, for the board approved their demands. Black students could immediately be admitted to Amarillo College.[3]

The first to enroll were all young ladies: Celia Ann Bennett, Freddie Imogene Jackson, Willetta Jackson (no relation), and Dorothy Reese. History at Amarillo College was made—and more quickly and easily than anyone might have expected. Certainly, this was not similar to later civil-rights battles in the South. More importantly, it involved no violence and hardly any resistance from the Amarillo College Board. The only real problem occurred when someone burned a cross on the campus. Willetta Jackson was terrified by the incident and has never forgotten it:

> I have never been [so] afraid as I was that day when the cross was laying on the ground burning. This is in my mind, just molded in my mind. It was a crisp October morning. I tell you I have never been as afraid in all my life. As I went across I started praying.[4]

It could have been a prelude to more incidents, but it was not, because of the long years of good race relations that Bones and others had been cultivating. Without downplaying Willetta Jackson's real fears, it can be claimed that Amarillo College was successfully integrated in 1951.

With this historic decision, Amarillo College became the third school of higher education in Texas to desegregate.

The University of Texas was under a court order to admit Herman Sweatt Toits to its law school, and Wayland College was the first school, public or private, to enroll black students in "regular undergraduate classes."[5]

Meanwhile, Amarillo High School went through a partial desegregation when some black students were permitted to take certain classes that were not available at Carver High. This was probably a result of the delegation to the Amarillo College Board.

Bones was already buried by the time all of this occurred and didn't get to see it, but he had always believed it would come and also much more. Those in the community understood that even after Bones' death, his lifelong work had prepared the way for these successes and others to come, and they intended to keep his name alive. Bones Hooks Day continued for a time, and he was honored time and time again at benefits and dinners to raise money for various causes. The Lobo Club led the way in keeping Bones' name alive. When it sponsored the youth club in 1953, there was a testimonial dinner in the name of the "beloved Negro cowboy" to help make final payments on the Bones Hooks Youth Center, a project that had begun in 1948. They held another testimonial in cooperation with the Panhandle Old Settlers Association in 1959 to raise funds for the Bones Hooks Memorial.

However, a memorial would not be completed until the 1970s. A pavilion honoring the bronc buster was suggested for the 1976 bicentennial festival, and a fashion show was held at the North Heights Park (so named in 1950, when the city of Amarillo took possession) to kick things off. The state panel awarded the festival chairman, Bill Harvey, with funding, some of which was designated for the Bones Hooks Memorial Pavilion Project. The pavilion was completed in 1978 and placed in the former North Heights Park, which was now officially renamed the Bones Hooks Park, as it should have been. That brought things full circle, except for one thing. Bones is not in the Great Westerners Hall of Fame, but that oversight is certain to be rectified, as new efforts to get him admitted are going forward as this book goes to press.

Now, it would not be right to conclude this book without enjoying some of Bones' quotes one more time. In this one, Bones was giving a blessing at one of the cowboy reunions:

> Lord God, you know us old cowhands is forgetful. Sometimes, I can't remember what happened yestiddy. We is forgetful. We just know daylight and dark, summer, fall, winter and spring. But I sure hope we never forget to thank you before we is about to eat a mess of good chili. . . . Chili eaters is some of Your chosen people. We don't know why You so doggone good to us. But Lord, don't ever think we ain't grateful for this chili we about to eat. Amen.

Bones' Life, in His Own Words

"Mr. Donald drove some cattle to Henrietta and left me there with them. I stayed and called Henrietta home. Well, it was just before this that I got the nickname 'Bones.' . . . I ain't never been able to get rid of that name yet and I'm seventy years old."

"It's a good plan to investigate before you make up your mind about folks that others are calling names."

"In the pioneer days there wasn't much race feeling. . . . When a man rode up to a door, no one looked at his color."

"If a man was man enough to work on a ranch in the early days, he was too much of a man to abuse me. If he did, I knew he wasn't man enough to stay there for long."

"They used to tell me that I couldn't stay in this country, that they wouldn't let a Negro stay. But I did not believe that and that is the reason I'm here . . . and I still don't believe it."

"You can keep friendship always. You may lose everything, but you can't lose that. There will be nothing in the world like old friends. . . . If a man loves his country and has faith in his country, it will bring him comfort, life and friends."

"The Panhandle has the finest families of any place in the country. . . . Congenial relations have been built up because of the type of white men living here."

"I have tried to be Indian and I have tried to be white. I got a strain of white blood in me, but my skin is colored. . . . I ain't ashamed of my color anymore. Now I'm satisfied to be what God made me, but I'll always see white and think white."

"There was just something between us. I knowed I was colored. He couldn't take me to his friend's house to visit and he couldn't show me his friend's sweetheart's picture. Just then I knew I was colored and he was white."

"Some colored people are envious of my position among white people. They doubt me; they are not in accord with me. They follow me because they know I can get help from the white people, but they do not trust me. Someday, they will understand me."

"I wanted our people to have an exclusive town and show the white man we could live as decent law abiding citizens so that when a black man committed a crime that the white man couldn't say all darkies were alike."

"If I want to help my people, I must remain with them."

"I wish to pay a tribute of respect to you with a lone white flower, a guerdon of honor, that one of our group has been sending for the past forty-eight years in honor of the pioneer men and women who have helped build this great empire of ours here on the Plains. For it is women of your type and organizations of this kind that can make a Democracy live, and it is one of the traditions of the Plains to give honor to whom honor is due."

"I want to extend my best wishes to all the good people of

the Panhandle, particularly the old-timers and pioneers who made this country and whose ranks are so rapidly diminishing. . . . A Merry Christmas to all the good white faces from the first old black Polled Angus that ever strayed into the herd."

"In the old days, no one asked a man his name or where he was from. He was just accepted as a man, a friend."

"I now spend my time looking after the pioneers."

"My word. I gave my word I'd have his money today. . . . Of course, I know I'm going to die. But don't worry. I feel wonderful."

Notes

Chapter 1

1. Bones Hooks, "Tales of the Life of a Colored Man in West Texas Pioneer Days," interview by Mattie L. Grant, Works Progress Administration (WPA), September 11, 1939, Panhandle-Plains Historical Museum, Canyon, Tex.; Jean Ehly, "Bones Hooks of the Panhandle," *Frontier Times*, July 1963, pp. 20-21.

2. Hooks, interview by Grant; "The Porter Doffed His White Coat for a Few Minutes," *Amarillo Daily News*, August 4, 1948; "'Bones' a 'White Spot' in Area's Civilization," *Amarillo Globe-News Bicentennial Edition*, 1976.

3. Bones Hooks Scrapbook (his personal collection of newspaper articles, interviews, letters, photographs, and other memorabilia now kept in the Amarillo Public Library); J. W. Baker, *A History of Robertson County, Texas* (Waco: Texian Press, 1970), 132-38.

4. Hooks, interview by Grant; Barbara C. Spray, ed., *Texas Panhandle Forefathers* (Dallas: National ShareGraphics, 1983), 75.

5. Hooks Scrapbook.

6. Hooks, interview by Grant.

7. Ehly, 20; Hooks Scrapbook.

8. John Denny Parker, *Historical Collections of Robertson County, Texas* (Salado, Tex.: The Anson Jones Press, 1955), 150; Henry E. Chatfield, "Bose Ikard, Top Hand," *The Real West,* December 1968.

9. Bones Hooks, "Recollection of Early Day Texas," interview by A. B. Hays, July 15, 1935, Panhandle-Plains Historical Museum, Canyon, Tex.

10. Ibid.

11. C. A. Bridges, *History of Denton County* (Waco: Texian Press, 1978), 143-44.

12. Hooks Scrapbook.

13. Ibid.

14. Ibid.

15. Hooks, interview by Grant.

16. Hooks Scrapbook.

17. Hooks, interview by Grant.

18. William Charles Taylor, *A History of Clay County* (Austin: Jenkins, 1974), 46.

19. Hooks, interview by Hays.

20. Ibid.; Ehly, 20.

21. Willie Newbury Lewis, *Between Sun and Sod* (Clarendon, Tex.: Clarendon Press, 1938), 145-47.

22. Ibid.

Chapter 2

1. Hooks Scrapbook.

2. Alton Hughes, *Pecos: A History of the Pioneer West,* vol. 1 (Seagraves, Tex.: Pioneer Book Publishers, 1978), 19-21.

3. Bones Hooks, "Old Bones," interview by History Class 413, April 16, 1933, Panhandle-Plains Historical Museum, Canyon, Tex.

4. Hooks Scrapbook.

5. Hooks, interview by Grant.

6. Paul H. Carlson, ed., *The Cowboy Way* (Lubbock: Texas Tech University Press, 2000), 17; Sarah R. Massey, ed., *Black Cowboys of Texas* (College Station: Texas A&M University Press, 2000), 195; J. Evetts Haley, *The XIT Ranch of Texas* (Norman: University of Oklahoma Press, 1958), 76.

7. Hooks, interview by Grant.

8. Ehly, 20.

9. Massey, 164-65, 195-96, 200.

10. Ibid., 195-200; Phillip Durham and Everett L. Jones, *The Negro Cowboys* (New York: Mead and Dodd, 1967), 109-11.

11. Hooks, interview by Hays.

12. Ibid.

13. James M. Oswald, "History of Fort Elliott," *Panhandle-Plains Historical Review (PPHR)*, 1959, pp. 57-58.

14. Pauline Durrett and R. L. Robertson, *Panhandle Pilgrimage* (Canyon, Tex.: Staked Plains Press, 1976), 243-47.

15. Ibid., 254-58.

16. Virginia Browder, *Donley County: Land of Promise* (Quanah-Wichita Falls, Tex.: Nortex Press, 1975), 89-91; Pauline Durrett and R. L. Robertson, *Cowman's Country* (Amarillo: Paramount, 1981), 92-93; Lewis, 145; Durham and Jones, 24; Millie Jones Porter, *Memory Cups of the Panhandle Pioneers* (Clarendon: Clarendon Press, 1945); 174; Ernest R. Archambeau, "First Federal Census of the Texas Panhandle—1880," *PPHR*, 1950, pp. 25-32.

17. J. Evetts Haley, *Charles Goodnight: Cowman and Plainsman* (Norman: University of Oklahoma Press, 1949), 242.

18. Hooks Scrapbook.

19. Ibid.

20. Hooks, interview by Grant.

21. Massey, 229; Hooks Scrapbook; Hooks, interview by Hays.

22. Hooks Scrapbook.

23. Hooks, interview by History Class 413.

24. James R. Gober and B. Byron Price, ed., *Cowboy Justice* (Lubbock: Texas Tech University Press, 1997), 83-88.

25. John L. McCarty, *Maverick Town: The Story of Old Tascosa* (Norman: University of Oklahoma Press, 1946), 129-39.

26. Hooks, interview by Grant.

27. Ibid.; "W. H. Fuqua—Business Genius," *Amarillo Sunday News and Globe Anniversary Edition*, 1938.

28. Hughes, 303-6.

29. Hooks Scrapbook.

30. Ibid.

31. Ibid.

32. Harley True Burton, *History of the JA Ranch* (New York: Argonaut, 1966), 26; Robertson, *Panhandle Pilgrimage*, 152-54.

33. Hooks, interviews by Grant and Hays.

34. Hooks Scrapbook.

35. Massey, 232.

36. Hooks Scrapbook.

37. Robertson, *Cowman's Country*, 92-95.

38. Ibid., 134-35; Browder, 80.

39. Laura V. Hamner, *Short Grass and Longhorns* (Norman: University of Oklahoma Press, 1943), 115.

40. Ibid., 109.

41. Hooks Scrapbook.

42. Spray, 285-86.

43. Ibid., 76; St. Stephens Baptist Church, Clarendon, Tex.; Hooks, interview by Hays.

Chapter 3

1. Haley, *Charles Goodnight*, 243; Robertson, *Cowman's Country*, 92; Massey, 166, 193-94.

2. Archambeau, 25-32.

3. Hooks, interview by History Class 413.

4. Lewis, 150-51.

5. Hooks Scrapbook.

6. Hooks, interview by History Class 413.

7. Ibid.

8. Hooks Scrapbook.

9. Ibid.

10. Ibid.

11. Hooks, interview by Grant.

12. Ibid.

13. Hooks, interview by History Class 413.

14. Hooks Scrapbook.

15. Ehly, 20-21.

16. Hooks Scrapbook.

17. Massey, 211.

18. Charles Warford, interview by author, February 18, 1998.

19. Hooks Scrapbook.

Chapter 4

1. Hooks Scrapbook.

2. Ibid.

3. Hooks, interview by History Class 413.

4. Hooks, interview by Grant; "Bones Hooks Left His Mark on Frontier West's Lore," *Amarillo Globe-Times,* November 14, 1973.

5. Gary Nall, "The Farmer's Frontier in the Texas Panhandle" *PPHR,* 1972, p. 5.

6. Jan Blodgett, *Land of Bright Promise* (Austin: University of Texas Press, 1988), 44.

7. Ibid., 97.

8. Ibid.

9. Hooks Scrapbook.

10. Ibid.

11. Hooks, interview by Hays.

12. Hooks Scrapbook.

13. "Rites for Bones Hooks Scheduled Monday at 2," *Amarillo Daily News,* February 4, 1951.

14. U.S. Bureau of the Census, *The Twelfth Census of the U.S., 1900; The Thirteenth Census of the U.S., 1910; The Fourteenth Census of the U.S., 1920,* Texas Population Statistics (Washington, D.C.).

15. Oscar D. Shorten, interview by author, March 21, 1997, Panhandle-Plains Historical Museum, Canyon, Tex.; Juell Shorten Nutter, interview by author, June 13, 1996, Panhandle-Plains Historical Museum, Canyon, Tex.

16. Hooks, interview by Grant.

Chapter 5

1. U.S. Bureau of the Census, *The Fourteenth Census of the U.S., 1920.*

2. *Texas Almanac and State Industrial Guide 1850-1990* (Dallas: Dallas Morning News, 1992), 163-78.

3. Laura V. Hamner, "Bones Hooks and His Modern Pioneers," *St. Louis Post-Dispatch,* May 14, 1947.

4. Spray, 155; Carrie P. Hines, *History of Mt. Zion Missionary Baptist Church 1910-1968* (Amarillo: Mt. Zion Missionary Baptist Church, 1968).

5. Della Tyler Key, *In the Cattle Country: History of Potter County* (Quanah-Wichita Falls: Nortex Offset, 1972), 286.

6. Ibid, 188-277.

7. Hamner, "Bones Hooks."

8. H. V. McSwain, interview by author, September 3, 1997, Panhandle-Plains Historical Museum, Canyon, Tex.

9. Planning, Zoning and Development Commission of the City of Amarillo, plats of the North Heights Addition, Miller Heights Addition, and Mathew Hooks Subdivision.

10. Hamner, "Bones Hooks."

11. McSwain, interview.

12. "Civic Body in Opposition to Negro Section," *Amarillo Daily News,* March 23, 1927.

13. "Northside Club in Interesting Meeting," *Amarillo Daily News,* December 4, 1912.

14. "Civic Body."

15. Potter County Clerk, *Deeds of Records,* Amarillo, 126-584, 162-210, 163-635, 174-431.

16. Ibid., 188-277.

17. Mrs. Wendell (Georgia) Faulks, interview by author, December 28, 1999, Panhandle-Plains Historical Museum, Canyon, Tex.

18. Hamner, "Bones Hooks."

Chapter 6

1. Hooks Scrapbook.

2. Ibid.

3. Robertson, *Panhandle Pilgrimage,* 320-21.

4. "Race Feeling Stirred Since Family Murder," *Amarillo Daily News,* July 7, 1927.

5. "Riots Lead to Arrest of Whites and Flight of Negroes, *Amarillo Globe-News,* August 16, 1927.

6. Julia Williams, interview by author, August 10, 2000; "Negro Home Bombed," *Amarillo Daily News,* September 9, 1929.

7. Hooks, interview by Grant.

8. J. L. Langston, letter to Bones Hooks, circa 1948, Hooks Scrapbook.

9. Amarillo Public Schools, letter to Bones Hooks, February 24, 1928, Hooks Scrapbook.

10. St. John's A.M.E. Church, Amarillo.

11. "The Fighting Mayor of Amarillo," *Texas Federation News,* March 1938, p. 2.

12. Ibid., pp. 2-5.

13. Spray, 77.

14. "Veteran Negro Cowhand Has Pitched Last Camp; Dreams Come True in North Heights," *Amarillo Daily News,* May 5, 1929.

15. Ibid.

16. Spray, 77.

17. "Negroes Not to Vote Here in Primaries," *Amarillo Daily News,* July 17, 1928.

18. "Ten Negroes Are Refused Ballots Here" and "Few Counties Admit Blacks," *Amarillo Daily News,* July 24, 1932.

19. *Texas Almanac and State Industrial Guide 1850-1990,* 187; U.S. Bureau of the Census, *The Fifteenth Census of the U.S., 1930,* Texas Population Statistics (Washington, D.C.).

20. Faulks, interview.

21. Ibid.

22. Sally Ruth Boaz, "History of Amarillo" (master's thesis, West Texas A&M, 1950), 43-44, 54-61.

23. "Bones Speaks His Mind on Proposed Museum Before Mike," *Amarillo Globe-News,* May 29, 1930.

24. Joseph A. Hill, *The Panhandle-Plains Historical Society and Its Museum* (Canyon, Tex.: WTAMU College Press, 1955), 65.

25. "Negro Takes Stand in Own Defense for Cowboy Murder," *Amarillo Daily News,* June 4, 1931.

26. Ibid.

27. "Flees to Jail After Verdict Was Surprised," *Amarillo Daily News,* June 6, 1931; "New Witness Testifies in Murder Trial," *Amarillo Globe,* June 6, 1931.

28. Nutter, interview.

29. Needlecraft and Art Club, letter to Bones Hooks, May 17, 1928, Hooks Scrapbook.

30. Hill, 132.

31. "Old Bones Loose Herds Negro Old-Timers into Pioneer Hall Round-Up," *Amarillo Globe,* June 9, 1933.

32. Ibid.

33. Hooks Scrapbook.

34. Ibid.; "Mathew Hooks Monument Club," *Amarillo Daily News,* May 21, 1933; Spray, 76.

35. "Mathew Hooks Monument Club."

36. Ibid.

37. R. B. Searcie, ed., *The Progress Magazine,* 1950, p. 8.

38. Nutter, interview.

39. "Ellington Matinee Red Letter Event for Negroes Here," *Amarillo Globe,* November 9, 1933.

40. Hooks Scrapbook.

41. Nutter, interview.

42. Jess Cortez, interview by author, April 29, 1998, Panhandle-Plains Historical Museum, Canyon, Tex.

43. "Negro Boys to Have Maverick Club Soon," *Amarillo Daily News,* July 12, 1934; "Story of 'Bones Hooks'—Negro Pioneer of the West—Is Saga of Respect for Men Who Have Achieved Highly and Well," *Dalhart Texan,* September 1, 1936.

44. "Dedication Honors Hooks," *Amarillo Daily News,* August 27, 1978.

45. "Mathew 'Bones' Hooks, a Mentor for the Children," *Amarillo Globe-News,* February 2, 2000.

46. Ibid.

47. Ibid.; "Emmett Galloway Has Busy Sundays," *Amarillo Globe-News,* November 9, 1934.

48. "Mathew 'Bones' Hooks, a Mentor."

49. Ibid.

50. Ibid.

51. U.S. Bureau of the Census, *The Sixteenth Census of the U.S., 1940,* Texas Population Statistics (Washington, D.C.).

52. "Pleas Made for Negro Aid," *Amarillo Daily News,* August 7, 1935.

53. "Dogie Club Boasts 1935 Perfect Mark," *Amarillo Daily News,* December 30, 1935; Potter County Public Schools superintendent, letter to Bones Hooks, October 30, 1936, Hooks Scrapbook.

54. McWhorter Milner, letter to Bones Hooks, Sons of Confederate Veterans General Headquarters, Richmond, Va., September 18, 1935, Hooks Scrapbook; Winnie Booth Kernan, letter to Bones Hooks, United Confederate Veterans General Headquarters, New Orleans, La., September 13, 1935, Hooks Scrapbook.

Chapter 7

1. David L. Nail, *A Short Sleep Past* (Canyon, Tex.: Staked Plains Press, 1973), 45-46.
2. "Dusters Blamed for Drought of 1934; 96 Sandstorms in Vicinity in 17 Month Period," *Amarillo Daily News,* January 1, 1935.
3. "Negro Open Forum Donates to Fund for Hungry Pupils," *Amarillo Daily News,* March 26, 1936.
4. "Negroes Ask for Road," *Amarillo Daily News,* March 15, 1936.
5. "Negroes to Celebrate Addition Anniversary," *Amarillo Globe-News,* August 30, 1936; Spray, 76.
6. J. O. Wyatt, letter to Bones Hooks, September 22, 1936.
7. "Bones Hooks Sends Greetings to All," *Amarillo News and Globe,* December 26, 1936.
8. "Funeral Director Remembers Early Years in City," *Amarillo Globe,* May 26, 1983.
9. Cleve Austin, interview by author, February 14, 1998, Panhandle-Plains Historical Museum, Canyon, Tex.
10. Ibid.
11. McSwain, interview; Warford, interview; Amarillo Hudspeth's City Directory, 1930-56.
12. Nail, 144-47; Eleanor Roosevelt, letter to Bones Hooks, April 16, 1938, Hooks Scrapbook.
13. Vice-Chamber Office, letter to Bones Hooks, March 7, 1933; U.S. House of Representatives, letter to Bones Hooks, April 16, 1933, Hooks Scrapbook.

14. Hooks Scrapbook.

15. Miles Bivins, letter to Bones Hooks, April 24, 1940, Hooks Scrapbook.

16. Austin, interview.

17. Cortez, interview.

18. "Service Is Given Negro and Is Not Demanded of Him," *The Catholic Register,* November 2, 1941.

19. Ibid.

20. Ibid.

21. Spray, 77.

22. Nutter, interview; Mrs. K. O. Hines, "Mrs. L. A. Shorten," n.d.

23. Warford, interview.

24. Austin, interview.

25. Civil Defense Control Center, letter to Bones Hooks, September 30, 1942, Hooks Scrapbook.

26. Bones Hooks, letter to Myrtle Volgamore, February 12, 1943.

27. U.S. Civil Service District, letter to Bones Hooks, March 10, 1943.

28. Bones Hooks, letter to Officer In Charge of Negro Troops, Amarillo Air Base, July 27, 1943, Hooks Scrapbook.

29. O. C. Barnard, letter to Bones Hooks, Fort Knox, Ky., September 8, 1943, Hooks Scrapbook.

30. Hooks Scrapbook.

31. Potter County grand jury signatures, April 9, 1945, Hooks Scrapbook.

32. Bones Hooks, letter to Frank and Myrtle Martin, December 27, 1944.

33. Bones Hooks, letter to the Western Cowpunchers Association, August 22, 1946.

Chapter 8

1. Potter County and Randall County Appraisal District,

Wyatt Memorial Hospital, 901 North Hayden Street, Amarillo, 1941-45.

2. Hooks Scrapbook.

3. Amarillo Negro Business League, letter to the public, circa 1941.

4. "Bones Hooks' Many Friends Offering Aid," *Amarillo Daily News,* October 31, 1950.

5. "Death Takes Bones Hooks," *Amarillo Daily News,* February 3, 1951.

6. "Trouble Bars Way As Bones Heads Down Last Trail," *Amarillo Daily News,* October 20, 1950.

7. "Death Takes Bones Hooks."

8. Spray, 76; Ehly, 22; "Lone White Flower Marks Final Rites for Pioneer," *Amarillo Daily News,* February 6, 1951.

9. Ibid.

10. Ibid.

Conclusion

1. Joe F. Taylor, *The AC Story: Journal of a College* (Canyon, Tex.: Staked Plains Press, 1979), 61.

2. Ibid., 62.

3. Ibid., 63.

4. Willetta Jackson, interview by author, November 5, 1998, Panhandle-Plains Historical Museum, Canyon, Tex.

5. Joe F. Taylor, 63.

Bibliography

Amarillo Public Schools. Letter to Bones Hooks. February 24, 1928. In Bones Hooks Scrapbook.

Archambeau, Ernest R. "First Federal Census of the Texas Panhandle—1880." *Panhandle-Plains Historical Review* (1950).

Austin, Cleve. Interview by author. February 14, 1998, Panhandle-Plains Historical Museum, Canyon, Tex.

Baker, Inez. *Yesterday in Hall County, Texas.* Memphis: The Book Craft, 1940.

Baker, J. W. *A History of Robertson County, Texas.* Waco: Texian Press, 1970.

Barnard, O. C. Letter to Bones Hooks. Fort Knox, Ky., September 8, 1943. In Hooks Scrapbook.

Bivins, Miles. Letter to Bones Hooks. April 24, 1940. In Hooks Scrapbook.

Blodgett, Jan. *Land of Bright Promise.* Austin: University of Texas Press, 1988.

Boaz, Sally Ruth. "History of Amarillo." Master's thesis, West Texas A&M, 1950.

"'Bones' a 'White Spot' in Area's Civilization." *Amarillo Globe-News Bicentennial Edition* (1976).

"Bones Hooks Left His Mark on Frontier West's Lore." *Amarillo Globe-Times* (November 14, 1973).

"Bones Hooks' Many Friends Offering Aid." *Amarillo Daily News* (October 31, 1950).

Bones Hooks Scrapbook. Amarillo Public Library.

"Bones Hooks Sends Greetings to All." *Amarillo News and Globe* (December 26, 1936).

"Bones Speaks His Mind on Proposed Museum Before Mike." *Amarillo Sunday Globe-News* (May 29, 1930).

Bridges, C. A. *History of Denton County.* Waco: Texian Press, 1978.

Browder, Virginia. *Donley County: Land of Promise.* Quanah-Wichita Falls, Tex.: Nortex Press, 1975.

Burton, Harley True. *History of the JA Ranch.* New York: University Microfilms, 1966.

Carlson, Paul H., ed. *The Cowboy Way.* Lubbock: Texas Tech University Press, 2000.

Chatfield, Henry E. "Bose Ikard, Top Hand." *The Real West* (December 1968).

"Civic Body in Opposition to Negro Section." *Amarillo Daily News* (March 23, 1927).

Civil Defense Control Center. Letter to Bones Hooks. September 30, 1942. In Hooks Scrapbook.

Cortez, Jess. Interview by author. June 6, 1996, Panhandle-Plains Historical Museum, Canyon, Tex.

Cortez, Jess, Scott Cortez, and Claude ("Sandy") Cortez. Interview by author. April 29, 1996, Panhandle-Plains Historical Museum, Canyon, Tex.

"Death Takes Bones Hooks." *Amarillo Daily News* (February 3, 1951).

"Dogie Club Boasts 1935 Perfect Mark." *Amarillo Daily News* (December 30, 1935).

Durham, Phillip, and Everett L. Jones. *The Negro Cowboys.* New York: Mead and Dodd, 1967.

"Dusters Blamed for Drought of 1934; 96 Sandstorms in Vicinity in 17 Month Period." *Amarillo Daily News* (January 1, 1935).

Ehly, Jean. "Bones Hooks of the Panhandle." *Frontier Times* (July 1963).

"Ellington Matinee Red Letter Event for Negroes Here." *Amarillo Globe* (November 9, 1933).

"Emmett Galloway Has Busy Sundays." *Amarillo Globe-News* (November 9, 1934).

Faulks, Mrs. Wendell (Georgia). Interview by author. December 28, 1999, Panhandle-Plains Historical Museum, Canyon, Tex.

"Few Counties Admit Blacks." *Amarillo Daily News* (July 24, 1932).

"The Fighting Mayor of Amarillo." *Texas Federation News* (March 1938).

"Flees to Jail After Verdict Was Surprised." *Amarillo Daily News* (June 6, 1931).

"Funeral Director Remembers Early Years in City." *Amarillo Globe* (May 26, 1983).

Gober, James R., and B. Byron Price, ed. *Cowboy Justice.* Lubbock: Texas Tech University Press, 1997.

Haley, J. Evetts. *Charles Goodnight: Cowman and Plainsman.* Norman: University of Oklahoma Press, 1949.

———. *The XIT Ranch of Texas.* Norman: University of Oklahoma Press, 1958.

Hamner, Laura V. "Bones Hooks and His Modern Pioneers." *St. Louis Post-Dispatch* (May 14, 1947).

———. *Light 'N Hitch.* Dallas: American Guild Press, 1958.

———. *Short Grass and Longhorns.* Norman: University of Oklahoma Press, 1943.

Hill, Joseph A. *The Panhandle-Plains Historical Society and Its Museum.* Canyon, Tex.: WTAMU College Press, 1955.

Hines, Carrie P. *History of Mt. Zion Missionary Baptist Church 1910-1968.* Amarillo: Mt. Zion Missionary Baptist Church, 1968.

Hines, Mrs. K. O. "Mrs. L. A. Shorten" (n.d.).

"History Makers of the High Plains." *Amarillo Globe-News* (May 14, 2000).

Hooks, Bones. Letter to Frank and Myrtle Martin. December 27, 1944. In Hooks Scrapbook.

———. Letter to Myrtle Volgamore. February 12, 1943.

————. Letter to Officer in Charge of Negro Troops, Amarillo Air Base. July 27, 1943. In Hooks Scrapbook.

————. "Old Bones." Interview by History Class 413. April 16, 1933, Panhandle-Plains Historical Museum, Canyon, Tex.

————. "Recollection of Early Day Texas." Interview by A. B. Hays. July 15, 1935, Panhandle-Plains Historical Museum, Canyon, Tex.

Hooks, Bones. "Tales of the Life of a Colored Man in West Texas Pioneer Days." Interview by Mattie L. Grant, Works Progress Administration (WPA). September 11, 1939, Panhandle-Plains Historical Museum, Canyon, Tex.

Hughes, Alton. *Pecos: A History of the Pioneer West.* Vol. 1. Seagraves, Tex.: Pioneer Book Publishers, 1978.

Jackson, Willetta. Interview by author. November 5, 1998, Panhandle-Plains Historical Museum, Canyon, Tex.

Kernan, Winnie Booth. Letter to Bones Hooks. United Confederate Veterans General Headquarters, New Orleans, La., September 13, 1935. In Hooks Scrapbook.

Key, Della Tyler. *In the Cattle Country: History of Potter County.* Quanah-Wichita Falls, Tex.: Nortex Offset, 1972.

Langston, J. L. Letter to Bones Hooks. Circa 1948. In Hooks Scrapbook.

Lewis, Willie Newbury. *Between Sun and Sod.* Clarendon, TX.: Clarendon Press, 1938.

"Lone White Flower Marks Final Rites for Pioneer." *Amarillo Daily News* (February 6, 1951).

McCarty, John L. *Maverick Town: The Story of Old Tascosa.* Norman: University of Oklahoma Press, 1946.

McSwain, H. V. Interview by author. September 3, 1997, Panhandle-Plains Historical Museum, Canyon, Tex.

Massey, Sarah R., ed. *Black Cowboys of Texas.* College Station: Texas A&M University Press, 2000.

"Mathew 'Bones' Hooks, a Mentor for the Children." *Amarillo Globe-News* (February 2, 2000).

"Mathew Hooks Monument Club." *Amarillo Daily News* (May 21, 1933).

Milner, McWhorter. Letter to Bones Hooks. Sons of Confederate Veterans General Headquarters, Richmond, Va., September 18, 1935. In Hooks Scrapbook.

Nail, David L. *A Short Sleep Past.* Canyon, Tex.: Staked Plains Press, 1973.

Nall, Gary. "The Farmer's Frontier in the Texas Panhandle." *Panhandle-Plains Historical Review* (1972).

Needlecraft and Art Club. Letter to Bones Hooks. May 17, 1928. In Hooks Scrapbook.

"Negro Boys to Have Maverick Club Here Soon." *Amarillo Daily News* (July 12, 1934).

"Negro Home Bombed." *Amarillo Daily News* (September 9, 1929).

"Negro Open Forum Donates to Fund for Hungry Pupils." *Amarillo Daily News* (March 26, 1936).

"Negro Takes Stand in Own Defense for Cowboy Murder." *Amarillo Daily News* (June 4, 1931).

"Negroes Ask for Road." *Amarillo Daily News* (March 15, 1936).

"Negroes Hold Annual Meet." *Amarillo Globe* (December 13, 1935).

"Negroes Not to Vote Here in Primaries." *Amarillo Daily News* (July 17, 1928).

"Negroes to Celebrate Addition Anniversary." *Amarillo Globe-News* (August 30, 1936).

"New Witness Testifies in Murder Trial." *Amarillo Globe* (June 6, 1931).

"Northside Club in Interesting Meeting." *Amarillo Daily News* (December 4, 1912).

Nutter, Juell Shorten. Interview by author. June 13, 1996, Panhandle-Plains Historical Museum, Canyon, Tex.

"Old Bones Loose Herds Negro Old-Timers into Pioneer Hall Round-Up." *Amarillo Globe* (June 9, 1933).

Oswald, James M. "History of Fort Elliott." *Panhandle-Plains Historical Review* (1959).

Parker, John Denny. *Historical Collections of Robertson County, Texas.* Salado: The Anson Jones Press, 1955.

Phillips, O. B. Letter to Bones Hooks. 1953. In Hooks Scrapbook.

Planning, Zoning and Development Commission of the City of Amarillo, plats.

"Pleas Made for Negro Aid." *Amarillo Daily News* (August 7, 1935).

Porter, Millie Jones. *Memory Cups of the Panhandle Pioneers.* Clarendon: Clarendon Press, 1945.

"The Porter Doffed His White Coat for a Few Minutes." *Amarillo Daily News* (August 4, 1948).

Potter County and Randall County Appraisal District, Wyatt Memorial Hospital, 901 North Hayden Street, Amarillo, 1941-45.

Potter County Clerk. *Deeds of Records.* Amarillo.

Potter County grand jury signatures, April 9, 1945, Hooks Scrapbook.

Potter County Public Schools superintendent. Letter to Bones Hooks. October 30, 1936. In Hooks Scrapbook.

"Race Feeling Stirred Since Family Murder." *Amarillo Daily News* (July 7, 1927).

"Riots Lead to Arrest of Whites and Flight of Negroes. *Amarillo Globe-News* (August 16, 1927).

"Rites for Bones Hooks Scheduled Monday at 2." *Amarillo Daily News* (February 4, 1951).

Robertson, Pauline Durrett and R. L. *Cowman's Country.* Amarillo: Paramount, 1981.

—————. *Panhandle Pilgrimage.* Canyon, Tex.: Staked Plains Press, 1976.

Roosevelt, Eleanor. Letter to Bones Hooks. April 16, 1938. In Hooks Scrapbook.

St. John's A.M.E. Church, Amarillo.

Searcie, R. B., ed. *The Progress Magazine* (1950): 8.

"Service Is Given Negro and Is Not Demanded of Him." *The Catholic Register* (November 2, 1941).

Shorten, Oscar D. Interview by author. March 21, 1997, Panhandle-Plains Historical Museum, Canyon, Tex.

Spray, Barbara C., ed. *Texas Panhandle Forefathers.* Dallas: National ShareGraphics, 1983.

"Story of 'Bones' Hooks—Negro Pioneer of the West—Is Saga of Respect for Men Who Have Achieved Highly and Well." *The Dalhart Texan* (September 1, 1936).

Taylor, Joe F. *The AC Story: Journal of a College.* Canyon, Tex.: Staked Plains Press, 1979.

Taylor, William Charles. *A History of Clay County.* Austin: Jenkins, 1974.

"Ten Negroes Are Refused Ballots Here." *Amarillo Daily News* (July 24, 1932).

Texas Almanac and State Industrial Guide 1850-1980. Dallas: Dallas Morning News, 1992.

"Trouble Bars Way as Bones Heads Down Last Trail." *Amarillo Daily News* (October 20, 1950).

U.S. Bureau of the Census. *The Eleventh Census of the U.S., 1890; The Twelfth Census of the U.S., 1900; The Thirteenth Census of the U.S., 1910; The Fourteenth Census of the U.S., 1920; The Fifteenth Census of the U.S., 1930; The Sixteenth Census of the U.S., 1940,* Texas Population Statistics. Washington, D.C.

U.S. Civil Service District. Letter to Bones Hooks. March 10, 1943.

U.S. House of Representatives. Letter to Bones Hooks. April 16, 1933. In Hooks Scrapbook.

"Veteran Negro Cowhand Has Pitched Last Camp; Dreams Come True in North Heights." *Amarillo Daily News* (May 5, 1929).

Vice-Chamber Office. Letter to Bones Hooks. March 7, 1933.

"W. H. Fuqua—Business Genius." *Amarillo Sunday News and Globe Anniversary Edition* (1938).

Warford, Charles. Interview by author. February 18, 1998.

Williams, Julia. Interview by author. August 10, 2000.

Index

Virginia Military Institute,
125
Volgamore, Myrtle, 164

W Ranch, 66
Waco, Texas, 154-55
Waddill, Geo. M., 124
Wade, J. W., 181
Walker-Warford Mortuary,
142
Wamba, 43
War of 1812, 52
Ware family, 112
Warford, Charles, 86, 142,
144-45, 163
Washington, D.C., 166
Washington, George, 48
Watley, Clarence, 125, 155
Watley, Jennie, 155
Watley Hotel, 155
Watley Mansion, 155
Watson, C., 127
Weatherby, Frank, 120-21
Weatherford, Texas, 25
Wellington County, 120-21
West Texas A&M, 108
West Texas Teachers
College, 130
West Virginia, 86
Western Cowpunchers
Association, 170-71

Weymouth, Chanslor, 137
Whaley, Henry A., 32
White, Benjamin Horton,
46
White, Frank, Sr., 67
White Caps of Sand Gall
Gizzard, 43
White Deer ranch, 55
Whittington, J. O. and
Maude, 108, 110, 114
Wichita Falls, Texas, 32, 125
Wild Horse Lake, 38, 108
Williams, A. J., 136
Williams, Flynn, 127
Williams, Joe, 67, 180
Williams, Red, 76
Williams, W. S., 180
Wilson, J. W., 180
Woods, Tiger, 155
Working Men's Social Club,
155
Wyatt, J. O., 152-53, 158,
161, 175-76, 180-81
Wyatt, Lavernia, 152
Wyatt Memorial Hospital,
175, 177

XIT Ranch, 36, 39, 48, 56,
85-86, 96, 151

Yellow House Canyon, 38